Children of Revival

Letting the Little Ones Lead

Vann Lane

Revival Press

An Imprint of
Destiny Image® Publishers, Inc.
P.O. Box 310
Shippensburg, PA 17257-0310

ISBN 1-56043-699-9

For Worldwide Distribution
Printed in the U.S.A.

First Printing: 1998   Second Printing: 1998

This book and all other Destiny Image, Revival Press, and Treasure House books are available
at Christian bookstores and distributors worldwide.

For a U.S. bookstore nearest you, call **1-800-722-6774**.
For more information on foreign distributors,
call **717-532-3040**.
Or reach us on the Internet: **http://www.reapernet.com**

Acknowledgments

To my wife Dana, my daughters Casey, Molly, and Whitney, and my son Joshua Vann. Ours is a family ministry, and God has blessed me with a wonderful and supportive family team.

To my parents, Niza Lane and the late E.V. "Pete" Lane, for living a godly example before me and never giving up on me.

To Pastor John Kilpatrick, who would not take no for an answer. Because of his persistence, I am blessed to be in the middle of possibly the greatest outpouring of God's Spirit in this century.

To Jim Wideman, for seeing something in me that I could not see myself, and then pouring himself into me.

To Jeremiah Oswald, a living example of what a child can become if he will but "seek first the kingdom of God." Watching Jeremiah seek after God's plan for his life is much of what this book is about.

To the ministry team of Kingdom Kids, the Children's Ministry of Brownsville Assembly of God. Children and adult workers alike, God is using you powerfully.

To Dian and Barry Layton, who gave inexhaustibly to the completion of this book.

To Don and Cathy Nori, Don Milam, Geoff Crawford, and the team at Destiny Image Publishers for making this book possible. You are true visionaries for the cause of Christ.

Endorsements

The cry of my heart for more than 20 years has been that children need to have a genuine encounter with God. They need to *know* Him, not just know *about* Him. In Vann Lane I hear a similar heart cry, and through his ministry I see a marvelous demonstration of God's *answer* to that cry. This book, like Vann himself, is honest, uncluttered, easy to understand, and filled with the profound truths that are only seen in the faith of children and the childlike. As a result of reading these pages, you will understand how the youngsters in your world can truly *know* God and how they can join the growing number of "children of revival."

Dian Layton
Author, International Speaker

Throughout Church history, children have been profoundly affected by revival. I have seen the Holy Spirit move on children of all ages in remarkable ways. Many churches couldn't understand how small children could receive radical preaching and be empowered with the Holy Spirit. In some of these churches the anointing on the children died down soon afterwards. Their people said, "If it was really God, it would have lasted!" but these churches were *not* providing a new *wineskin* in which the youngsters could develop their spiritual potential. *Children of Revival* tells the incredible story of a church in the Brownsville community of Pensacola, Florida, that was hit by revival and had no alternative but to change their *wineskin*. Since then, not only the adults, but also the children have been affected by God's Presence in wonderful ways. *Children of Revival* is an excellent book. I thoroughly recommend it. Pastor Vann Lane has a wonderful story to tell and great insights to share. Not only should this book be in the hands of all parents, children's pastors, and teachers, but every senior pastor must read it as well. The only limitation that children have, is what we adults put on them. I, for one, believe that God has ordained that the children will lead many of us into revival.

David Walters, President
Good News Fellowship Ministries
Macon, Georgia

Contents

Foreword

When revival broke out on Father's Day, 1995, one of the things that immediately caught my attention was how the children were powerfully impacted. It reminded me of the Scripture in Matthew 21 when the children were crying in the temple and saying, "Hosanna to the son of David!" Jesus responded by quoting Psalm 8:2: "Out of the mouth of babes and sucklings Thou hast perfected praise" (Mt. 21:16). The children had discernment of the works of Christ and responded by praising Jesus.

As I beheld the children on Father's Day, I knew that they discerned what was happening was of God because they were crying and worshiping—something I had never seen before. Since Father's Day, 1995, hundreds of children have been baptized and thousands of children have come to be in God's Presence. They see visions and they prophesy. God is using the children in ways I never imagined. Joel prophesied that God would pour out His Spirit upon our sons and daughters (see Joel 2:28). It should be no surprise.

Vann Lane was placed by the Holy Spirit in the position of Children's Pastor shortly before revival broke out. His tender and innovative leadership has been a haven for the children to flourish in as they come under his guidance. In the Children's Ministry, they have mini revival services, and they learn to worship, to pray for one another, and how to be used and led by the Holy Spirit. In his book, *Children of Revival*, you will weep as you see Joel's prophecy coming to pass right before your very eyes.

God has chosen Vann Lane to be a leader in these last days and to focus on a neglected area of our ministry—our children. Children touch all of our hearts and they move us as nothing else does. Allow Vann Lane's book *Children of Revival* to move you to allow the children to move into ministry. It could change your ministry, your church, and even your home. "Out of the mouths of babes and sucklings is praise perfected."

John Kilpatrick, Pastor
Brownsville Assembly of God

Part 1

And Then Came Revival

Chapter 1

We're Moving to Pensacola

"Thank You, Jesus! A Children's Pastor!"

The entire Children's Ministry department of Brownsville Assembly of God in Pensacola, Florida, took one look at me, packed up their few belongings, and ran to the sanctuary.

And I was left standing there...alone.

With a brave sigh I squared my shoulders and decided to inspect the condition of things. I looked in the supply closet. Three forlorn puppets looked back. I walked into the Children's Church meeting room. On the platform was a PVC pipe puppet stage leaning slightly to one side and tied precariously to the wall. I walked into the nurseries and was met with water dripping from the ceiling into puddles on the faded blue carpet.

Refusing to be daunted, I thought to myself, *No problem. I am prepared. I can handle this. I have been trained and I know exactly what to do. I'll have things in shape right away! Pastor said to go ahead and get everything I need. I'll just order in all the props and costumes and stuff and....*

And then the Lord interrupted me, speaking very clearly to my heart.
"No.
You will not.
I want to do something different here."

Prior to coming on staff at Brownsville, my wife, Dana, and I and our three daughters, Casey, Molly, and Whitney, attended Evangel Temple Assembly of God in Montgomery, Alabama. There the Lord had drawn me to Jim Wideman, a veteran Children's Minister. Jim saw in me what I had not previously recognized—a person who would do well working with children. He pulled me under his wing and mentored me for two years.

I was always a church-goer and grew up in a godly family. When I was a child, I even had a position in the church—my position was to sit still and be quiet. I was baptized at the age of eight, but it was meaningless to me.

For years Dana and I, without knowing it, dabbled in God's plan for our lives. I believe that God has a destiny for every human being, but it isn't until we give our lives to Him that our eyes are opened to see it. The call to Children's Ministry was always there; we just didn't realize it for what it was. I was actually teaching a Sunday school class of three-year-olds when, at 32 years of age, I finally understood and experienced a relationship with Jesus.

Dana and I got married at the ages of 18 and 19 years old. I met her the year before she graduated from high school in Tallahassee, Florida, and I knew she was to be my wife. Our relationship must have been ordained by God, for Dana put up with me through some very difficult years. I attended

Florida State University and was the drummer of a rock and roll band for many years. I remember countless nights when the guys and I would sit around smoking, drinking, and rock and rolling while Dana curled up and went to sleep in the middle of it all.

After college I became a salesman for the Bridgestone Tire Company. I traveled and lived in bars during the week and went home on weekends. I had everything I wanted—a high-paying job, a nice house, and new cars. I loved new cars. Recently Dana and I counted up 29 cars we had during a period of 22 years. When I turned 16, the first thing I did was get my hands on a steering wheel.

But the cars and the house and all the things didn't bring the happiness we had expected. A growing emptiness was within us. My lifestyle during the week was taking its toll. My heart grew cold to the fact that I had a family. I just didn't care about what happened in my home. The very odd thing about those years is that we still went to church on Sundays. We went through the motions like we were supposed to, but there was nothing there.

One of the places I traveled to was Pensacola, Florida. Eddie Tisdale was one of my contacts there with Bridgestone Tire. For over a year, Eddie talked to me about his church and his pastor. Eddie knew the lifestyle I was in and that I needed the Lord. I kept putting him off, telling him that I would go with him "one of these days." Eddie never gave up on me. He kept asking me to his church and telling me how great his pastor was.

One night in May, 1988, I went to the condo where I stayed when I was in Pensacola. I plopped down on the sofa and turned on the TV to a program called *In Times Like These.* There on the screen was Eddie's pastor, John Kilpatrick. With mild interest, I began to listen to his sermon. "If Jesus Christ came back tonight, where would you be?" he challenged. "If tomorrow never happened, where would you be?"

For the next month I thought about those words. Finally I came to the understanding that I needed the Lord and didn't have Him. I always thought I had Him. I experienced water baptism when I was eight years old. I attended church my whole life. Now, at the age of 32, I realized that none of it had ever been real to me.

One of my biggest concerns is that children all over this nation and all over this world are being taught that all they have to do is say a prayer; all they have to do is get baptized. I tell children that the waters of baptism will not save them. Saying the words of a prayer will not guarantee that they are going to Heaven. Children need to understand that they must make a personal commitment to God; they must have a personal relationship with Jesus Christ. I don't want them to grow up like I did—all dressed up and going through the motions on Sunday, but living an altogether different program Monday through Saturday. I don't want the children whom I have contact with to live their lives thinking they are saved when in fact they are not.

The last night I can remember living the old life, I was staying with friends in one of the bay areas between Pensacola and Mobile. At ten o'clock that evening a couple of inebriated friends and I got into a boat and headed for a well-known night spot. The boat was a super high performance model, and we were skimming across the water in the darkness at about 70 miles per hour. Suddenly, words from

John Kilpatrick's sermon came to my mind: "If tomorrow never happened, where would you be?" A sense of fear came over me and I remember whispering, "Lord, You get me out of this one, and I'll never do this again." I recall going into the lounge and realizing it was over. I just knew that bar would be the last one I would ever walk into.

That was a Thursday night. The next morning I got into my car and headed home. I walked into our house and our next-door neighbor, Ruth Wegenhoft, was about 15 minutes behind me. Ruth had been talking to us, and on a regular basis, asked about our relationship with God. "Are you right with the Lord? Are you sure?" I would nod my head in response. "Oh, yes. No doubt about it. I am right with the Lord." Now, here was Ruth at my door.

She looked at me. "You are ready to make a commitment to Jesus Christ," she said.

"Yes, Ma'am," I responded, "I am." And we prayed.

Therefore if any man be in Christ, he is a new creature: old things are passed away; behold, all things are become new (2 Corinthians 5:17).

I remember lying in bed the next morning, talking to God. "I'm going to be a better person, Lord. I don't want the bar scene anymore. I don't want the alcohol anymore. I don't want the partying and rock and roll." I opened my eyes to see Dana looking at me with a puzzled expression on her face.

"What in the world has happened to you?" she asked. She could see a visible difference in me.

Over the next weeks, Dana continued to watch me. Then one evening she called me into the kitchen. All the alcohol in our home was on the counter. "We're going to have a party!" she announced.

I shook my head, "No. You know I'm not going to drink with you."

"You'll like this party," she said. She began to uncap the bottles and started pouring our whole stock down the drain.

But that wasn't enough. We went into the living room and began to pull out records. I used a screw driver to scratch the albums and Dana pulled out the insides of tapes. We wanted to make sure that no one else would pick them up and be influenced by that music. We went through every area of our lives and cleaned house. Steve Hill, the evangelist who speaks every revival night at Brownsville, preaches on a regular basis about "cleaning house." Getting rid of sin in our lives is a constant process. We began that night and we've been cleaning ever since.

Dana and I grew restless in the denominational church we were attending. We became aware of it's social club kind of atmosphere and the uncomfortable way people looked at us when we started bringing our Bibles to church. We started going to Evangel Temple Assembly of God and began to feel something we had never felt before—the realness of Christ. (Ironically, I met the pastor of my former denominational church a few years ago at a funeral. He walked over to me and said, "I just thought I would let you know I have joined your profession. I'm a salesman now. I sell insurance." I said, "Well, I'm not a salesman anymore. I've joined *your* old profession. I'm a pastor.")

I was still traveling, and if I was within an hour's drive of Pensacola, I would go to the mid-week services at Brownsville

Assembly. Meanwhile, our Sunday attendance at Evangel was a totally new experience for Dana. I remember her saying, "Okay, I'll go; but I'm not going to lift my hands." In the middle of the worship service, they began to sing one of her favorite hymns, "Holy, Holy, Holy." I looked over at Dana out of the corner of my eye. Her hands went up and tears flowed from her eyes. After the service we walked out and got into the car. I didn't say a word to her. Finally she said, "Well, I lifted my hands, but I'm not going to speak in tongues!" (Actually, it was a very short time later that both Dana and I released the Holy Spirit and spoke in tongues.)

The call to full-time ministry came to us as a couple, but separately. I love how God does that kind of thing. He spoke to me in an audible voice one night in a hotel room. It was as clear as any voice I have ever heard. "Sell everything you have," He said, "And follow Me." I was so excited! I wanted to get home and tell Dana about my experience—but when I walked into the house, she couldn't wait to tell me something. We almost had a battle over who was going to get to talk first! Then I just blurted out, "The Lord told me last night to sell everything we have and follow Him."

Dana turned as white as a sheet. She had heard the same words the night before while in Savannah, Georgia, visiting her mom. We immediately put a "For Sale" sign in our front yard.

We felt that we were about to explode in our desire to serve the Lord full-time, but we waited two years before God opened the door. During that time I was promoted in my job. I was the number one salesman of the nation for a year and a half, which meant added bonuses and commissions. God was preparing us. He was helping us to change our life priorities and to get out of debt. He was laying the foundation, and when the time came for us to take the step, it was not difficult.

It was during those two years that Jim Wideman mentored me in Children's Minstry at Evangel Temple. I will always be thankful to Jim for recognizing God's hand on our lives and for his input and training. Shortly after Jim left Evangel, I was hired on as the Children's Pastor. Dana and I and our three daughters were excited and content. We had a ministry with about 300 puppets and 8 full-body costumes. We had "flash pots" on the corners of the stage, a confetti cannon in the back, laser lights that danced all over the room, and a sound system that would blow the walls down. Anything that you could ask for to entertain boys and girls, we had it. For the next two years, we were in a growing church with a growing Children's Ministry. We loved it.

At the beginning of 1994, a twinge of restlessness entered my spirit. I tried to shake the unsettledness aside, but instead of leaving, the feelings began to intensify. I remember one Sunday after church sitting with Dana in our car before driving out of the parking lot. "I'm not sure how to explain this," I said, "but I feel like I've led this group of children as far as I can lead them."

Shortly after that day, John Kilpatrick called us.

John Kilpatrick has referred to me as his trophy. Whenever I visited Brownsville, he introduced me to people as his trophy because of the lifestyle I had been in until the night I heard him preach. (Since Father's Day, 1995, John Kilpatrick has accumulated thousands of trophies!) I had kept in touch with Pastor John, and whenever I had an opportunity to be in Pensacola, we would get together for lunch.

Now here he was calling me to come to Brownsville as the Children's Pastor. Neither Dana nor I had any desire to leave Evangel. Despite the fact that the waves of restlessness in my spirit were becoming increasingly frequent, I didn't want to acknowledge them. I was in a nice little comfort zone and I wanted to stay there. "Sorry, Pastor John," I responded, "I don't think the Lord is calling us to leave here. Things are going too good." Then, for some reason, I added, "But listen, if you can't find anybody, call me and we'll talk some more."

He called me every week.

My inner restlessness grew into feelings of separation from Evangel and the ministry there. I spoke of these feelings to Dana, but she was not interested in leaving. She had, and still has, some very close friends in Montgomery, Alabama. She home schools our three daughters and was part of a very tight home school support group. Finally she agreed to our meeting with John Kilpatrick, but she was adamant: "This is not of God!"

The night we got home after our meeting with John Kilpatrick in Brownsville, Dana continued reading her Bible long after I had fallen asleep. Verses 11 and 12 of Ezra chapter 9 stood out to her, and she began to weep. Verse 11 speaks of God leading His people into a land that is unclean and polluted. When we had driven down the streets of Pensacola, Dana had gotten the girls to put their heads down so they wouldn't see the violence and perversion pictured on the streets, billboards, and store windows.

Verse 12 goes on to say that God's people would be strong and eat the good of that land, and that it would be an inheritance for their sons and daughters. She began weeping so loudly that I woke up, concerned. "What's wrong?" I asked.

She shoved her Bible toward me and pointed to the Scripture. "Read this!" I looked at the words, puzzled. Waking up out of a deep sleep like I did, those verses weren't particularly meaningful to me. She grabbed back her Bible and snapped, "God is not having to deal with you like He's having to deal with me!"

I knew we were going to Pensacola.

But I didn't know the great adventure God had planned for all of us.

Chapter 2

Father's Day, 1995, and Beyond

All the adult Children's Ministry workers at Brownsville had fled to the sanctuary—but one turned around and came back. Jerry Henrikson has been faithful to this day. He's been my right arm—I really don't know what I would have done without him. Jerry and Dana and I—we're "The Team." Our three daughters were the puppeteers for the three puppets.

It was May, 1994, and we began with a Children's Church of 60 or so boys and girls. I prayed for laborers, but my prayers went unanswered. At least, I thought they did. It took me awhile to recognize the ministry team God was sending me. The 11- and 12-year-olds began to line up at my door. Prior to my coming, these children had stopped attending Children's Church because of their boredom and disillusionment. But now, here they were. "Anything I can do to help, Pastor Vann?" Gradually the Lord revealed part of the new thing He wanted to do at Brownsville. Children's Ministry was to be just that—*children ministering*.

I began to assign small tasks to those 11- and 12-year-olds, and to my surprise, they proved faithful and very capable of doing the work. I gave them more things to do and more children their ages began to hang around. (I will share more specifically on how our children are doing the work of the ministry in a later chapter.)

With my growing team in place in Children's Church, I began to deal with the facility issues. This was a very real concern in the nursery area, where the rain still formed puddles on the faded blue carpet. The nurseries were across the street in the old building. I wanted to move them into the new building where they would be closer to the sanctuary, and where we could expand. The only way for us to do this, however, was to trade places with the adult Sunday school classes.

When I asked the adults to leave their fine classrooms and move to the less-than-fine area across the street, I was not the most popular person around Brownsville. Still, they got over it. It was amazing how quickly the leaky roof was repaired and the faded blue carpet replaced! This seemed to spark the much-needed renovation projects in other areas of the old building, including the office areas. Now in the midst of revival, we are very grateful for the Lord's hand in these practical areas of preparation.

From the rooms that previously were home to the adult Sunday school classes, we designed and built eight nursery areas for children from birth through five years of age. At the time, eight nurseries seemed unnecessary, but I felt that was what we were to do. (Now we actually need to add 4 more to make a total of 12!) We decorated the walls and made each room fun and special.

After I had been at Brownsville almost a year, we moved our 150 children into the cafeteria area, which comfortably seats 300. (Presently, our regular attendance is 350 plus, and we are preparing to move to another new area with a seating capacity of 600.) I thought again of all the "stuff" I would buy—the fancy props and gadgets I was used to in my teaching style with children.

When I first went on staff, Pastor John had given me complete clearance to go ahead and purchase everything I needed. He told me that I could have whatever it would take to build the Children's Ministry. He has been like that ever since. There has never been a need I have asked for that I didn't get. I have greatly appreciated this.

The financial resources were there, but again, I felt the Lord say, *"No. You are not going to do that here. I am going to do a new thing. I am going to do a new thing in this place."*

So we never got all the "stuff." We still don't have all the "stuff." I have come to the conclusion that God wants us to get out of the "stuff" business and get into the business of spending time with Him. The children of Brownsville Assembly have begun to experience the presence of God. I have also found that when God is around, you don't need all the fancy gadgets and Hollywood-style props to reach boys and girls for Jesus. The power of the Holy Spirit is all you need.

After relocating Kingdom Kids, the name of the Children's Ministry here at Brownsville, I had one remaining facility project on my list. We took the tiny room that had been the nursing mothers' room and turned it into a break area for our nursery workers. The new nursing mothers' room was a large and more comfortable area. (Now we are looking at yet another expansion because of the tremendous growth we have experienced.)

I remember the last Saturday we completed all the painting and decorating. I looked around with a feeling of satisfaction. Everything looked good; in fact, it looked great. I turned off the lights and went home. The next morning was Father's Day, 1995.

Pastor John Kilpatrick had been praying for revival. He longed for the Lord to move; he longed for the reality of God that had been instilled within him as a child. Pastor John sometimes tells the story of a late night prayer meeting that he remembers from childhood. It was about 12:30 a.m. and young John plus other members of the church were seeking God in the sanctuary. Although the front doors were locked and bolted shut, they suddenly flew open. Two ten-foot-tall angels came into the sanctuary. They said nothing. After a few moments they turned and left. That supernatural encounter left a lasting impact.

Pastor John cried out, "Where is the God of my childhood?" He would come into our church late at night, lie on a pew, and pray for revival. He rallied the church behind him, and we began to seek the Lord.

Our congregation met on Sunday evenings for two-and-a-half years specifically to pray for revival. When Pastor John first changed the Sunday night format from traditional preaching to a dedication to prayer, the attendance began to increase. Pastor John has testified that he actually was quite troubled by a fear that people would stop coming when he responded to God's command that Brownsville was to become a house of prayer. (See Mark 11:17.) He was concerned about how many people might not be able to move to the next step. He wondered how many people would hang on too tightly to their religious traditions and not be able to enter into the new things God wanted to do.

During Pastor John's time of walking this out as a step of faith, God revealed to him that, yes, Brownsville Assembly would lose people. The Lord told our pastor that we would lose hundreds, but we would gain thousands. The Lord said someday the night services at Brownsville would be more well attended than the Sunday morning services. Pastor John told the congregation these things, but certainly no one at that time could comprehend the magnitude of how this prophetic word would be fulfilled.

At that time we had a church of 1800. Today our membership is around 3500, and between 2,500 to 5,000 visitors attend each evening revival service. Since June of 1995, we have had more than 300,000 people come to the altar. We have tallied a very conservative estimate of 120,000 decisions for the Lord. We actually have a much higher number of written, signed forms, but we speak of a lower number so we can never be accused of exaggeration.

Until this time, our Sunday night prayer meetings were so powerful that, at times, people would weep before the Lord for the burdens God laid upon their hearts as well as for their unsaved loved ones. Pastor John had tapestried banners made that depicted prayer categories. These banners were stationed at various areas around the sanctuary as suggestions of categories to pray for. A banner for "Children" and another for "Families" were among them.

Steve Hill, who preached the Father's Day, 1995, services when revival broke out (and who has been preaching every revival service since), has testified about those banners. One night when he visited Brownsville a few months before Father's Day, he saw a young boy kneeling at the "Souls" banner, crying out to God. With tears streaming down his face, the child was beating on the floor and calling out to God for the salvation of his family. James 5:16 tells us that the earnest, heartfelt prayer of a righteous man is very powerful. Steve said that as he watched that little boy pray, he knew that God was soon going to move on Brownsville in a mighty way.

For two-and-a-half years the people of Brownsville interceded in prayer. We prayed for the fires of revival to fall on our church and around the world. We interceded for families to be healed and for lives to be restored. As we continued in prayer, everyone had a growing sense that something was coming, a sense that we were preparing for something big. The feeling of anticipation among the staff members was incredible. It was almost something you could touch.

Word got to us that God was moving in Toronto, Canada. We began hearing phenomenal reports of God's visitation there. We decided to go and see for ourselves if it was authentic revival.

In the spring of 1995, Dana and I, along with several other people from the Brownsville staff, visited Toronto Airport Christian Fellowship. Pastor John had planned to be with us, but then suddenly began having the symptoms of a heart attack. He didn't have a heart attack, but the situation prevented him from going on that trip.

Toronto was not at all what I expected—even though I didn't really know what to expect. After each service, people lined up along lines of tape on the floor, waiting to receive prayer. For the first day and a half, I hid behind the columns of the huge converted conference building, just watching. I had never seen anything like it in my life. People were laughing and shaking and carrying on—it both scared and impressed me. I was impressed most by the intense hunger of the people. They stood waiting in line for prayer with a kind of excitement and anticipation that I had not seen before. Gradually, my feelings of skepticism were replaced with a desire for that same intensity toward God, but I still held on to my determination to be in control of the situation.

I scanned the prayer team during that first day and a half, looking for the exact person I wanted to pray for me. One lady pastor who was visiting from a California Vineyard church stood out to me. I sensed a prophetic anointing upon her. Dana and I joined the crowds of people standing on the lines of tape and asked her to pray for us.

Down we went.

Some call it "going out in the Spirit"; some call it being "slain." Some children I know call it getting "zapped." All I knew was that it was God. A kind of sweet peace enfolded me. I was aware of the rest of the people around me, but felt in no hurry to try to get up. Dana and I both lay there "resting in the Spirit" for about 45 minutes. It was a truly beautiful encounter with His presence.

Our pastoral team then went home to Brownsville. None of us ever really talked about our experience to other church members; it was as if the Lord wanted us to be quiet about it. What we had seen was a genuine, authentic move of God. We had observed what revival looked like in Toronto, but we sensed that God wanted to do something different in our setting.

Over the past few years, each church I have visited that is moving in revival has a sense of uniqueness. It feels almost as though God is setting up spiritual hospitals; each one specializing in its own area of call and gifting, but each possessing the same dramatic reality of His presence. Authentic revival is breaking out across the globe.

It's real, folks. And it is absolutely life-changing.

On Father's Day, 1995, Steve Hill, a traveling evangelist and personal friend of Pastor John, preached the Sunday morning service. The power of God fell.

I missed that historic service because, of course, I was in Children's Church. But I knew something major was happening in the sanctuary. Usually the service was finished around noon. Not that day. I have a traffic light set up at the back of Children's Church for the television department to communicate with me the status of the service. The green light goes on when the sermon starts, the amber when the altar call starts, and the red when the people are dismissed.

That morning the green light went on about the normal time; about one hour later it turned to amber. I knew it was time to start winding down. To my amazement it switched back to green! Then it went to red. "Okay, boys and girls, it's time...oops!" The light went back to amber. Parents gradually drifted in to pick up their children, but instead of going home, most of them took their children with them back to the sanctuary! They tried to describe to me what was going on, but I just couldn't visualize it. This was no soft sweet visit from God; it sounded like a hurricane had hit the church!

The last parent came in around 4:00 p.m. The service had lasted six hours. It was, at that time, a record for Brownsville Assembly. Now three- and four-hour Sunday morning services are common. The evening revival services can last for eight hours. When you are really in the presence of God, who cares what time it is?

Steve Hill preached again that night. Again, the power of God fell on the congregation. People were falling; actually, it was more like they were being strewn all over the floor. The aisles were covered with crying, shaking bodies. These were people I knew—from elderly, mild-mannered deacons right on down through the ranks. People were unable to walk. In fact, they acted like drunkards. Our dignified Pastor John was draped, seemingly unconscious, over the steps of the platform. I watched in amazement.

Sadly, that is what I ended up doing for several months. I watched. I stood and observed from a distance.

When revival fell in Brownsville, a kind of controlling skepticism rose up in my heart. I like things to stay the same. This was all so strange to me, so I didn't jump right in. In fact, I resolutely resisted it. I was 100 percent behind what was happening, supporting it; I didn't mind working myself to death for it; but, I didn't want to get too close. The resistance in me grew into a critical spirit and a hardened heart, both of which I managed to hide from other people.

As time went on, I entertained thoughts of leaving and going to a different church, an "ordinary" church. I never shared these feelings with anyone, not even Dana. In the fall of 1995, a couple from Australia, Tony and Robyn Kassas, visited our church. One evening they ministered to our home school group. When prayer time came, I tried to leave, but Dana talked me into staying just to watch.

I knew those home school families personally. I knew their problems and struggles. Tony and Robyn began to speak words of knowledge and prophecy over them—specific, detailed words that I knew had to be from God. The critical skepticism I had felt toward them dissipated, and I let them pray for me.

Almost immediately, Robyn began to focus on the fact that I had been thinking about leaving Brownsville. I was impressed. Only God could have told her that. She went on to say that I was full of the Word of God. Now God wanted to move me into a place of balance. God wanted to bring a balance in my life between the Word and the Spirit, between Truth and the experiencing of that Truth.

I look back on that night as a major turning point for me. The fearful, critical skepticism was gone. I jumped into revival, and now I can't stop. My heart was changed, and my ministry changed as a result. Now, during those three- and four-hour Sunday morning services, we see the power of God touching the children.

When I'm on the prayer team in the sanctuary, I just can't stop praying for people. I see the hunger in people's faces. They want something from God, and I want to do all I can to help them receive from Him. In fact, the lights will start going out and I'm still there praying.

My beloved friend, Elmer Melton, is in charge of closing up the church after services. On Sunday mornings when he comes to close the Children's Church area, usually we're not finished yet, so he shrugs his shoulders and leaves it up to us to lock up. When I'm one of the last people praying for folks in the sanctuary, Elmer usually walks over to me with a smile on his face and says, "Hey! This is not Children's Church! Let's go home!"

Every week, I have the opportunity to speak to dozens, even hundreds, of Children's Ministers. I teach a (supposedly) one-hour class every Friday morning, which really lasts between two and four hours. I am very transparent with these people. I tell them how I am in the middle of revival—one of the largest revivals of the century—but when it first started, I was a critical, skeptical Children's Pastor with 60 or so children, 3 puppets, and 1 adult volunteer worker. That is inspiring to people! They say, "Look what God can do!"

Every week, I meet discouraged Children's Ministers who are trying to find answers. They feel desperate to have God move on their lives and the lives of the youngsters of their congregation. "But how can I do anything?" they wonder. "After all, I'm *just* a Children's Minister."

"*Just* a Children's Minister" is a statement that we need to address....

Chapter 3

"Just" a Children's Minister

"Just" a Children's Minister. These few words are more than a statement; they represent a philosophy, a belief system, that must be challenged and changed in both the ministers themselves and the Church as a whole.

People have asked me, "Vann, when do you think you will move on to be a youth pastor?" or, "Vann, how many years do you think it will be until you become a *real* pastor?" Why is it that Christians seem to think that the bigger people are, the more important the ministry is to them?

In the last chapter of the Gospel of John, Jesus said to Peter, "If you love Me, feed My lambs...if you love Me, feed My sheep." Feeding the young of the flock is a high and significant calling.

God has called me to pastor the children of Brownsville Assembly. I am committed to that calling. I feel very honored and very privileged to help lay foundations in the hearts of children, to teach them godly principles that will affect their lives—for eternity. I am not looking for some "greater" ministry. I have already found it.

I heard a prominent Children's Minister give an excellent message a few years ago about placing importance on the Church's ministry to children. He said that if you go to a steak house that has sharp knives, glass plates, and glass cups, you know that the restaurant is not really opening its doors to children. If you don't bring your children to dinner, then that's fine with them. It is obvious by the way the place is decorated—the kind of carpet on the floor and the china on the table—that it's fine with them if you leave your children at home with a baby-sitter.

This mentality can also be in the Church. "Leave your children at home with a baby-sitter," or, "We'll provide entertaining child care—just don't bring them into our fine sanctuaries where they'll scream and cry and throw up on the seats."

This man went on to say that steak houses make money and do well—but go to McDonalds and see what they do. When you walk in the front door, you see tables and chairs bolted to the floor. The pictures are bolted to the wall. They have plastic forks and knives and tile floors. At the end of the day, all those ice cream cones that were dumped upside down are washed out with a water hose. Like the steak houses, McDonalds makes money, but their money is taken to the bank in armored vehicles.

He said that the church that opens its doors to snotty-nosed little children with holes in their jeans will receive a great reward from the Lord. When you reach out to the ones who can't give you anything back, the Owner of the cattle on a thousand hills (see Ps. 50:10) will see that your needs are met. Matthew 10:42 says that if you give just a cup of cold water to a little one, you will have a reward.

The churches who place value upon their ministry to children, who make families feel welcome, are the churches that are exploding both numerically and in the blessing of God.

"Cleansing Stream," a program that comes out of Jack Hayford's church in Van Nuys, California, helps bring deliverance to Christians hindered by the enemy in any area of their Christian walk. During this video seminar at our church, I was asked to close one of the sessions. It was about word curses. So many of the things we say about people— ourselves, our spouse, our children, our church—are actually words that bring a curse.

Just before the session was over, I sat, microphone in hand, preparing to do the pastor role of directing the discussion time. A growing conviction was filling my heart. *"Just* a Children's Pastor…" I began to realize how often I had said that; how often I had spoken those words over the years and, most recently, during my Friday morning sessions with Children's Ministers. I began to realize that there is a kind of bitterness in the hearts of most Children's Ministers, which I had inadvertently helped to fuel with my own testimony of *"just working with the children at the end of the hall."*

I was the first person at the altar that evening. Instead of leading the discussion, I used the microphone to lead in a prayer of repentance for the words I had spoken that had brought a curse to my life and to the lives of other Children's

Ministers. Most of the people in the room that night joined me at that altar, confessing how they, too, had said things like, "I'm *just* a stay-at-home mom," or, "I'm *just* this or *just* that...." It was a very powerful evening.

Many Children's Pastors feel out of place in a church staff setting. They feel like outsiders. They may never speak to the Senior Pastor on a regular, one-to-one basis. In most cases the Senior Pastor has never walked into the Children's Church. Neither has the pastor's wife or any other people in church leadership positions taken the time to visit the young of the flock. They have heard that everything is going fine, and that's all they seem to care about.

Children's Pastors and volunteer ministers often feel disjointed from the rest of the body. Even in the midst of revival, they can feel alienated from the inner workings of the church. Very seldom are Children's Pastors seen on the main platform. Very seldom do they have the opportunity to share with the adult congregation what God has been doing in the lives of the children. The seeming lack of recognition and importance results in their being "just in Children's Ministry."

When I struggled with these kinds of feelings, I came to the realization that said, "Hey, who am I working for anyway? Who brought me to this church? Did a man call me, or am I here by divine appointment? Who am I really working for?" Children's Minister, I pray that the Lord will reveal to you your true purpose and identity. You need to understand that *God* has called you. He has put you in a place of divine responsibility and authority over the lambs of His flock.

One of the key principles I have learned through this revival is that the closer I get to God, the less I need or even desire the praise and recognition of people. In fact, I now shun these things. Revival turns everything right-side-up. When we fall in love with Jesus, we come to the place where we are satisfied. We come a place where we look at life with a new and correct perspective.

I believe that God wants us to view children with tender honor and monumental expectation. All people, especially children, will rise up to the levels of behavior and achievement we expect from them. Children who are constantly being ignored, put down, and criticized by adults will have great difficulty expecting anything different from God.

Many of us have made the mistake of getting into a pattern of devaluing children in one way or another. How many children have felt the sting of being ignored when they have tried to communicate with their parents or leaders? How many children have had their questions or opinions ridiculed? We must wake up to our tendency as adults to send messages to children that minimize their worth.

There are, of course, many ways we can send the correct messages to the little "walking video recorders" around us. Here are a few simple suggestions to help you honor children:

- Look into the eyes of a child when he or she is speaking to you. If you haphazardly nod your head, with your mind on some distant project, the child will feel your disinterest. Children miss very little.

- Acknowledge your faults to the children around you. Don't try to hide your imperfections and mistakes. Lead the children by your example of humility. Be able to say, "I'm sorry. I was wrong." As children see adults humbly admitting their shortcomings, they will see that it is safe to acknowledge their own sins and mistakes. That will, in turn, establish a pattern of having a soft heart to God. It will help them to build healthy relationships with people—both now and in the future.

- Be open and vulnerable concerning how God deals with you. Many times I share with the children on Sunday mornings about how I had to repent that week. God *always* challenges me on the very issues on which I am about to speak to the children. How can I possibly declare some scriptural truth with anointing and authority if that truth is not functioning in my own life?

I vividly remember what happened during a time I was preparing to teach about friendship. I had been going through a time of discouragement, and just before I left for church that Sunday morning a close friend of mine called to see how I was doing. God had awakened him about 3 a.m. that morning, telling him to pray for me. I told the children in Kingdom Kids how thankful I was that this fellow listened to the Holy Spirit's prompting.

I also told the children, with tears in my eyes, that I needed to repent for not being a good friend myself. In my discouragement, I hadn't even asked this fellow how *he* was doing. Then he told me that he had been diagnosed with having cancer of the pancreas. This was the third time in his life that my friend had received a cancer diagnosis. I was the first person at the altar that day to get prayed for. The boys and girls saw me crying, asking God to make me that kind of friend—someone who could reach out to others even when in the midst of personal crisis. Again, I found myself not alone at the altar. Almost everyone else in the room came forward too.

I believe that this type of vulnerability is honoring to children. We are showing respect to them when we share how God is dealing with us personally. Open honesty is a way to model the Christian walk. It is a way to show boys and girls that Christianity is a life of change, challenge, forgiveness, grace, and obedience to the conviction and leading of the Holy Spirit. Being a Christian means responding to the Word of God and allowing our character to be shaped by Him.

By saying that I am *just* a Children's Pastor, I am failing the volunteer workers who work alongside me. I am bringing the curse upon them of being *just* children's workers. And I am failing the boys and girls. I am putting them in a place of being *just* the children.

God has revealed to me that I need to assume the position of a children's advocate. I need to be a voice for them. I am in a position where I can defend and uphold them as equal citizens in the Kingdom of God. The little ones cannot speak up for themselves; so, I will speak for them. I will seek the Lord for creative ways I can set them before the congregation, not as the cute little kids, but as holy, anointed people God wants to use in these days.

Communication is so important. You can have the most fabulous things going on; you can have children moving powerfully in the Spirit; but it needs to be communicated. There must be an open communication between the Children's Minister and the Senior Pastor, and then that communication must also happen between the Children's Pastor and the congregation.

I can guarantee you that most pastors are not unwilling to let the Children's Pastor share with the congregation. They are not unwilling to hear testimonies of the exciting things happening in Children's Ministry. They *want* to know; they want to be aware and involved.

Children's Pastor, if you are feeling cut off, alienated, and ignored, it is not the pastor's fault...it's yours. It is a result of your own lack of faith and negative belief system of the importance of what you are doing!

Recognize the high calling that is yours and the value of the little ones whom He has called you to minister to! Be that advocate! Be that one who pushes through the crowd and brings the little ones to the place God wants them

Then they brought little children to Him, that He might touch them; but the disciples rebuked those who brought them. But when Jesus saw it, He was greatly displeased and said to them, "Let the little children come to Me, and do not forbid them; for of such is the kingdom of God. Assuredly, I say to you, whoever does not receive the kingdom of God as a little child will by no means enter it." And He took them up in His arms, put His hands on them, and blessed them (Mark 10:13-16 NKJ).

In her book, *Soldiers With Little Feet* (1989, 51-52), Dian Layton quotes these verses from Mark and then goes on to say this:

"The Lord has not changed. Hebrews 13:8 tells us that He is the same yesterday, today, and forever. That means it is still His desire to have the children brought close to Him.

It is still His desire to take them up in His arms and bless them.

"As we look at today's Church, I wonder if His present disciples have changed much, either. Are they still wanting to have the children held back in some corner while the adults meet with Jesus? (Ouch!) I feel that the Lord is looking today for some disciples who will realize His desire to touch the children—not just have them learning *about* Him—and who will do all they can to see His desire fulfilled!"

These are my feelings exactly. Children's Minister, you need to realize that when you are pushing Children's Ministry forward, you are not trying to promote yourself. You are trying to promote the little ones in your care. When I get assertive in the need for our congregation to know what God is doing in Children's Church, I am not trying to push Vann Lane forward. I am trying to make a way for the children. I don't want them held off in the back in some corner while the adults meet with Jesus.

Listen, if Jesus had that problem with His disciples, why are we surprised when people today still have those same attitudes toward children?

Here in Brownsville, we have the continual challenge of lack of space to accommodate the crowds of people. I remember one of the ushers telling me one time, "Pastor Vann, we're going to have to use the children's church area for overflow next week because it's Easter Sunday." I said, "Oh. And what are we going to do with the children?" His response now seems funny and hardly believable, but this is what he actually said, "Oh, they're not coming."

He had given no thought to what his decision meant: more than 300 children suddenly put out of their room. Over and over I have encountered a similar attitude. *"After all, they're just kids. You're just baby-sitting them anyway. Put them out in the grass, or take them out for ice cream. You'll think of some way to entertain them."*

Now, this usher is a fine person. He just exemplified an attitude that has permeated the Church. A favorite word in recent years has been *paradigm*. We desperately need a paradigm shift in our approach toward Children's Ministry. Recently, I spoke with a well-known and highly respected Christian leader. He said, "I've been thinking of all the wonderful testimonies of young people getting drastically changed by the Lord at Brownsville. God is saving them out of their lifestyle of drugs, alcohol, and sexual sin. When you think about it, isn't it a waste of time trying to reach children? I mean, is it really worth the effort? God will get hold of them when they are teenagers."

For several moments I felt stunned.

Then I said to him, "So you think that God is pleased with those baptismal testimonies?" He looked surprised and I continued, "Don't you think it would be a much better testimony to the Lord and to the world if we had a whole room full of young people who could say, 'There was never a time in my life when I didn't know Him'?"

He said, "Well, then why isn't that happening?" "Because the Church, for the most part, has not been reaching the children," I answered. "The Church has not been training and preparing them. The Church keeps the children off in some back room or basement area, and then they bring them out as teenagers whose lives are in a mess. At that point the Church shoves them off to the youth pastor who is expected to get them all saved and right with God, and then the Church shouts praises at their testimonies."

Christians, in general, have been programmed to believe that rebellious children and teenagers are normal. As a result, we have settled for far less than God's best for them. We have fed the children so much of the world and excluded them from the power and presence of the Lord. We must repent for not protecting the "ear gate" of our children, for allowing rock music to pump darkness into their hearts. We must repent for not protecting their "eye gates," for allowing them to view violent and sexual acts on television and in magazines. We must repent of our apathy and our self-centeredness and the lack of time we have spent with them and in prayer about them.

Somehow, there exists the mentality that children cannot possibly be touched by God in a real way. The Church's wrong belief system toward children has often resulted in the children being in the poorest facilities, lacking in necessary materials, and being led by people without training, help, or finances. Many parents are interested only in "dropping off" their children and rushing off to "get fed" without ever considering the spiritual appetite of their children. It amazes me, this attitude of some parents that says, "Here, take my kid for a few hours; I'm dropping him off. Maybe you can teach him something. Maybe he'll get saved. I hope so." No wonder the Church's children are so spiritually dead. Their inner man is not cultivated, nurtured, or fed.

People ask me the question, "What is revival, and how do I get it in our ministry to children?" A very real part of the answer is to say good-bye to past concepts and ways of doing things. Say good-bye to the days when Sunday school teachers and Children's Church workers simply taught their lessons, hoping that a seed was planted for the future. Say good-bye to the days when parents looked at Children's Ministry as a convenient drop-in baby-sitting service or, at best, a place where their child just might hear the gospel and get saved. Say good-bye to the days of desperate pleading for workers and then accepting just about anyone to work in children's ministries.

Here at Brownsville, there is never any solicitation for children's workers. People who feel that they are called to work in the area of Children's Church must take the initiative in approaching us; and now, in sharp contrast to the past, they are coming to us literally in droves.

Those who express an interest in working in Kingdom Kids are carefully screened and interviewed. They are asked to sit and observe for awhile before making any kind of commitment. We only want those people who are called by God to be there. It is a high calling to work with the young of the flock. We want shepherds, not hirelings.

I firmly believe that parents are the ones called by God to train up their children in the way they should go (see Prov. 22:6). I must offer the children something that their parents cannot if I am to justify taking them out of the sanctuary. In fact, we do not have Children's Ministry, except for nursery, during any of the evening revival services. I cannot duplicate what happens in the sanctuary, nor should I try. God is sending revival to His people of every age. What a joy it is to see both young and old receiving revival fire!

One goal I have for the children is to provide them with an evangelistic opportunity. I want to see them making an impact on their world now, through their words, choices, lifestyles, and testimonies. I want to see them reach people today who might not otherwise be touched by the gospel. How much suffering can be avoided if these children touch the children around them while they are still young and haven't yet been lured into the nets the devil has waiting for them?

Steve Hill often encourages people who attend the revival services with a quote from his mentor, Leonard Ravenhill: "The opportunity of a lifetime must be seized during the lifetime of the opportunity." I apply this thought to Children's Church every Sunday morning. In some cases, for a visiting child, that service may be the only one he or she will attend for a very long time. That little visitor may have been invited by one of the children in my care, or by someone who has been praying and is anticipating his or her friend to hear the gospel that morning.

What happens during those few hours in Children's Church may be the only opportunity visiting children have for years to come. My meeting must be both evangelistic and discipling. The spark of the Holy Spirit must be lit; hunger for God must be imparted. Each child must be given the opportunity to receive Jesus Christ as Savior. The course of a child's life could very well be changed forever as a result of that one service—not to mention the family and countless numbers of people whom that child will touch in the future.

Children's Minister, what you do has eternal consequences!

Another goal I have for Brownsville Assembly is that we will never have to go outside the church to find ministers in any area. We will never have to go out looking for video or sound technicians, or for musicians, ushers, or prayer warriors. When the children come up through the ranks of

Children's Church, they are being trained and prepared for ministry.

One Sunday morning a few months ago, I did an object lesson. I blew up a few balloons and then set a wooden plank on top of them. I asked one of the children to come and stand on the plank. Of course, it was a very wobbly place to try to stand. I went on to speak about the importance of building on a strong foundation so that our lives will be strong and unshakable.

As Children's Ministers, we are helping to lay the foundation stones that last for a lifetime. Will the children in your care live strong, unshakable lives as a result of the foundation you helped to lay?

"Just" a Children's Minister. Since I personally have been challenged to become more than *just* a Children's Minister, I am both very forgiving of this attitude and very adamant to change it.

Not for my sake, but for the sake of the children of revival.

Part 2

Letting the Little Ones Lead

Chapter 4

A Little Child Led Me

...a little child shall lead them (Isaiah 11:6).

When visiting parents and Children's Ministers come to observe our Sunday morning children's service, "Kingdom Kids," they are blessed to see how the children are moving in God.

We have some children who begin to intercede right at the start of the meeting and who are still interceding three and four hours later. Usually these children are taken to an area at the back of the room where they can yield to what God is doing without being distracted, or being a distraction. They cry and moan and tremble as the Holy Spirit prays through them (see Rom. 8:26). It is one of the most awesome things I have ever seen in my life.

Other children are involved in many areas of ministry. Some have ushering roles—greeting, maintaining order, etc. Our prayer team is made up entirely of children. These boys and girls pray for people at the end of the meeting and God flows through them in power. I have one elder in Children's

Church. Jacob Green was 11 years old when I set him in as an elder; he is 12 now. Jacob has a powerful anointing on his life to heal the sick. He is my elder. I will be setting more elders in place as time goes on.

Visitors ask me constantly, "How did you get the children to this place? How did you teach them to move in God like this?" My answer surprises people. It may surprise you.

I didn't teach them. Most of what I have done is get out of the way. They know what to do instinctively. I simply provide a place of safety and freedom for them to obey the Holy Spirit's prompting. I see my role as mostly that of a facilitator, of allowing the children to express the giftings God has put within them. About the only things I do on Sunday mornings is turn on the air conditioning, preach a little bit, and try to keep out of the way.

Children are ready for revival. Like their parents, children are tired of the phoniness of going through the motions of church attendance and outward religious expressions. They want to experience the reality of God in their lives. I have found, however, that *unlike* their parents, children are generally quick to recognize when God is moving and to simply jump in. It is as though they are little pieces of kindling. They catch fire more easily than the big old logs!

In addition to our three daughters, Dana and I have a beautiful little boy. Joshua Vann is a year-and-a-half old. I have noticed that when he is anywhere near a swimming pool, we have to fight to keep Joshua Vann out of the water. Children are drawn to the water as if drawn by a magnet. I've seen that same thing with the river of God. Children seem to recognize it very quickly and are drawn to it. They jump in with joyful abandonment. I love watching the children dancing around the sanctuary. I love the way they watch for the anointing; and when they see it, they run toward it.

Recently I was praying for Don Nori, the owner of Destiny Image, who published this book. There was an intense feeling of the presence of God. I opened my eyes to see about six children gathered around me, waiting for prayer. They recognized the power of the Holy Spirit and they wanted to get some for themselves! I love that about children. They look to see what is happening and then they run to it. They will get prayed for over and over and over again on any given night. Their hunger and desire for God is undeniable.

In the simplicity of their faith, children readily accept that God is all-powerful, and they usually take His Word quite literally. Their abilities to receive, to be equipped, and to give, go far beyond what we often give them credit for. Boys and girls can feel the war going on around and within them. They need to be equipped with the Word of God and the power of His Spirit to resist the temptation and deception of the enemy!

We need to affirm and challenge children in their ability to know God. Children have a marvelous capacity to have a relationship with the Lord. The Bible, in fact, tells us that they are an example to us! In Matthew 18:3, Jesus says that unless we become like a little child, we will never enter His Kingdom! God loves the faith of the little ones.

"How did you get the children to this place? How did you teach them to move in God like this?" If anyone has taught anyone around here, it has been the children teaching me.

As I mentioned earlier, I did not jump into revival. The first person in my family to enter into what God was doing was my eight-year-old daughter, Whitney. In the very early days of the revival, Whitney began to intercede and travail in prayer during the altar calls. Her body would violently shake from head to toe. Sometimes she wailed so loudly that you could hear her above Steve Hill. I am ashamed to admit this, but I didn't encourage Whitney; I actually tried to quench what she was doing. I was afraid and I didn't understand what was going on. I tried to make her stop, but the shaking and crying continued.

One night during a revival service, Whitney began to reach down to the ground with both hands and then lift her hands back up over one shoulder. She repeated this action over and over and over, all the while trembling and weeping. Dana looked at her, bewildered. "Dear God! What is happening to my child?!" Dana felt the Lord telling her that Whitney was, in a spiritual sense, reaching down and snatching people from hell. We watched with a mixture of awe and amazement.

At the end of the meeting, we asked Whitney what God had been saying to her while she interceded. What did it mean when she kept pulling her hands down low and then back up over her shoulder? Whitney's answer was a confirmation of what the Lord had already spoken to Dana. Our little girl had been snatching people from hell.

In October of 1995, Whitney shared her testimony of this experience during an evening revival service.

"God was telling me to take people off the earth where it was like they were living in hell, and to put them into a stage (a place) where they would live like Jesus on the earth. God told me that if I didn't snatch them out of hell

from the earth that they would go down to hell when they died. So I obeyed God and I pulled them up....

"Brother Dick Rueben prayed for me and all I could hear in my ears was God saying, 'Whitney, when you get older, you're gonna deliver My people'....

"As I reached down, I felt pain in my arms like people feel in hell. But as I reached up, it felt like God running through my arms. I felt love and joy and peace. It felt just wonderful because when I put them down I could just feel the pain that people feel when they go to hell..."

At this point in her testimony, Whitney bowed over low and began to weep. Pastor John came over to her and said gently, "Whitney, what would you want say to say to other children about this revival?"

Crying softly, her voice breaking, Whitney responded, "Listen to God when He talks to you so you can tell people what He's saying to you."

Pastor John went on to quote Joel 2:28 where it says God will pour out His Spirit and our sons and daughters will prophecy; they will speak for Him.

We believed, and still believe, that God would use Whitney in the future to deliver His people. We also believed that her intercession was definitely born of the Spirit and of great significance. We were about to find out how significant it was in the lives of one family.

JoAnn Lowell is a successful businesswoman who visited the revival. She loved it so much that she decided to stay! JoAnn's husband, Robert, came from their home in North Georgia to get his wife out of Brownsville and take her home. He came to save her from this "cult thing" she had gotten into. The night he showed up at church, JoAnn was on the platform giving her testimony. Robert decided then and there that he would file for a divorce.

With his heart filled with anger and remorse, Robert Lowell went to leave the building. In the foyer he ran straight into Steve Hill. Robert was trying to get out, but Steve thought he was coming toward him to get prayer; so he reached out his hand to pray for him. Although Steve's hand never even touched him, Robert was literally thrown back a number of feet against the wall by an invisible force.

When Robert Lowell got up off the floor, he was a changed man. He had a new understanding and respect for the power of God.

The Lowells moved to Pensacola and became members of our church. They fit right in and made friends easily with the Brownsville family. Robert seemed particularly drawn to our eight-year-old Whitney. Our daughter is a charming little girl and many people like to be around her, but this was unusual. He said, "I feel drawn to this child. I don't know why."

Then Robert saw a video of Whitney's testimony. As he watched, a sense of weakness went through his body. A feeling of realization filled him. "I was one of the people she was snatching out of hell. Whitney was praying for me. I just know it. That is why I've felt so drawn to her. Whitney saved my life."

Since that time we have grown to dearly love "Uncle" Robert and JoAnn. They are a continual blessing in our lives and to the Brownsville family, serving in many capacities. The Lowells have begun an evangelistic outreach called

"Awesome God Ministries" and have been speaking at numerous churches. As they minister, Robert usually gives his testimony. He testifies that it was the prophetic intercession of little Whitney that snatched his soul out of a life destined for hell and brought him into life in Jesus Christ.

The Lowells are producing a video of their story, which will include Whitney telling of her experience in intercessory prayer. Copies of the video, "Testimony of Whitney Lane," have been sent out all over the world. God has already been using her to deliver many of His people. I feel that God used her to help *deliver me* out of my religious state and set me more at ease with the extraordinary ways He was touching people.

A child who is totally yielded to the Holy Spirit has an intensely powerful effect on adults. On January 31, 1997, during an evening revival service, God used some children to influence the course of the meeting...

The presence of God was especially intense. It was thick. Steve Hill had given the altar call and hundreds of people had come forward to get their lives right with the Lord. Earlier in the meeting while on an errand, I had passed by a room down the hall and noticed a group of children playing. This room, where we offer supervision for boys and girls whose parents are working in some area of ministy, has been an on-going source of concern for me. I feel very strongly that children who are in the building need to be in the revival service, and that parents need to either serve on alternating nights or have their children be in the sanctuary under the care of a responsible adult.

That night, as the power of God swept through the service, I was especially grieved to think of those children playing and missing out on what the Lord was doing. I went back to the room down the hall. There was the television monitor with the service going on, but no one was watching it. Angie Griffin, an intercessor at our church who has a real heart for children, was one of the supervisors that night. I took her aside and explained how powerfully God was moving. I said, "You need to get the children to stop playing. Get them tuned into what the Holy Spirit is doing. You need to give an altar call in here tonight." Then I went back into the service.

Well, Angie did get those children focused, and she did give an altar call. To her surprise, the power of God began to move in that room! A group of about eight little girls began to intercede. When Angie realized the depth of what was happening, she took the girls into the sanctuary, where Robert Lowell "happened" to be ushering that night. Robert led them right into the middle of the room, and those little girls yielded to the Holy Spirit, crying out with tears and groanings. The whole church was interceding. Shortly after Angie and her "players-turned-*pray*ers" came into the meeting, Steve Hill asked people to be quiet while he spoke to them, and everyone went quiet.

Everyone, that is, except the eight little girls. They continued to cry and wail in prayer so loudly that they were a distraction. Angie tried to get them out of the sanctuary to an area where they could continue to pray without disturbing the meeting. The nearest place was the hallway behind the platform. She managed to get the shaking, weeping little group that far; then they fell under the power of God right there in the little hallway. An usher closed the doors on either end of the corridor to try and contain the wailing. Angie sent someone to get me so that I could see what was going on.

I opened the door to the hall and could not stand because of the presence of the Lord. I knew Pastor John needed to see this. I went and got him. He, too, could not stand because of the intensity of God's presence. Pastor John went back into the sanctuary and spoke to the people from Matthew 21:13-16 where Jesus said "My house shall be called the house of prayer," and "Out of the mouth of babes and sucklings Thou hast perfected praise."

Then Pastor John sent someone with a microphone to the little hallway. The heart-wrenching, anointed intercession of those eight little girls turned the church upside down. I had never before seen the power of repentance as it happened that night.

With the voices of the children wailing in the background, Steve Hill exhorted the congregation to believe for the salvation of their family members. "People are being birthed into the Kingdom right now," he said. He went on to lead in prayer for abused children—those who had been abused in the past and those who even that night were being molested and brutalized.

The spirit of intercession descended on the people. Brother Steve said, "If you have a problem with this kind of service, you need to look in the Bible. Read about the miracles and the signs and the wonders. Read about the earthquakes and the salvation conversions. Read about a typical day in the early Church."

Then Brother Steve said, "Strongholds were broken tonight." He asked for trash cans to be brought right up on to the platform and told people to get rid of the garbage in their lives, to get rid of anything that was drawing them away from God. People started dumping things out of their pockets, purses, and backpacks. They started going to their cars and getting magazines, books, and tapes that the Holy Spirit was convicting them about. They threw out drugs, cigarettes, lighters, pieces of clothing and jewelry. I watched as one young man took rings from various places on his face and threw them into the trash can. One woman came up and gave the keys to a house to one of the pastors. She had been using that house to have an adulterous affair with her boss for more than 13 years.

It was definitely a night for house cleaning—literally! God loves living in a clean house. A greater sense of His presence always sweeps in as a result of repentance. The anointing in the revival services is always greater when people cry out to God in repentance. The river flows with liberty when the trash in our lives is disposed of.

(This service was recorded. The video is called, "Lord Have Mercy II," and is available through our church.)

During the first months of the revival, children were experiencing the power of God in the sanctuary; however, we didn't see significant demonstration of His power in the children's meetings until God got hold of the Children's Pastor.

Revival didn't start moving in Children's Church until revival was moving in me.

When I finally "jumped into the river," we saw God begin to move powerfully in Kingdom Kids on Sunday mornings. The January 31, 1997, service was the definite source of a further spiritual breakthrough. After that meeting, intercession became a common occurrence, and intercession continues to usher in the outpouring of God's Spirit week after week after week.

God used, and has continued to use, the children to teach me powerful spiritual truths. He taught me an amazing lesson about deliverance through a little seven-year-old boy named David.

David came from a broken home. His father, a deacon in a church in a different county, left David's mother for another woman. David was devastated. He had such a spirit of rejection that no one could touch him. He wouldn't stay in school; he was constantly getting into fights. His face was clouded, sullen, and angry. I was not trained in deliverance, but I knew that is what David needed.

One Sunday morning I noticed a group of children around David. He was crying, and I wondered if he had gotten hurt somehow. I hurried over and, to my surprise, David was not hurt; he was being ministered to. A little girl was praying softly and rubbing his head. One little boy was gently holding his hand. "David doesn't feel like he has any friends," one child told me. "He thinks that no one likes him."

I felt this was the open door to David's heart that I had been waiting for. While Jerry and Dana closed the meeting and greeted the parents as they came to pick up their children, I very gently took David by both hands and began to speak to him, but David pulled away. Each time I tried to touch him, he would jerk away. Just about then David's mother, a member of the intercessory prayer team, came into the room. As she went to try to calm her son, the Spirit of the Lord said very clearly to me, "If he would just hug you...."

I said, "David, would you come over here?" David shook his head. "David, come hug me. Let me hug you." I reached out and tried to gently draw him toward me. He pulled away with such force that he fell onto the floor, where he curled up into a little ball.

I went over and quietly lay down right beside him on the floor. For the next two-and-a-half hours David's mom and two other intercessors and I stayed with him. I just wouldn't quit until this got dealt with. Even though she was an intercessor, David's mother hadn't realized the depth of her son's anguish, or its source, until that morning. Then, when she heard him growling at me, that lady started to pray. By this time I was up off the floor and standing on my feet. One of the other intercessors, Chris Meier, started to pray and wave her arms like she was trying to push back demonic forces surrounding the boy. Suddenly, David let out a cry and lunged at me. He threw his arms around my neck and hugged me, sobbing. Chris let out a victorious scream.

David is a transformed little boy. Now on Sunday morning he serves in a variety of areas and intercedes powerfully; he also is the "catcher" for my elder, Jacob. While Jacob prays for children to be healed, David stands behind the little person, praying softly. If the presence of God touches the child and he or she falls, David gently lowers the child to the floor. A few months ago David was a withdrawn, sad, angry little boy who wouldn't let anyone near him. Now he is reaching out to people, his face shining with the glory of God.

That was a classic example of how God and the children have been teaching me, how the Holy Spirit has been giving guidance as we obey Him, one step at a time, in areas that are new to us. In this generation, the children we are called to minister to are more in need of deliverance than any previous generation. I constantly meet hurting, abused, and even suicidal youngsters. I know one 11-year-old girl who tried three times to kill herself. She has taken pieces of glass to cut her skin, trying to sacrifice herself to the devil. This generation of children is in desperate need. Only a loving, supernatural encounter with the living God will set them free.

This generation is crying, "There must be more! There must be more power, more truth, more miracles, more love! There must be more than the misery and emptiness and despair I see around me." One way or another our children will be driven to fill the void that cries out within them—a void only God can fill. If we are lukewarm in our guidance in the areas of faith and perseverance with God, the enemy of their souls will certainly boldly take full advantage of our slumber and ensnare the little ones around us.

In recent years, the Church as a whole has relied on attention-getting programs and the promotional strategies of the secular world to increase attendance. In many instances, ministries for all ages have fallen into reliance upon entertainment, programs, and special events because they have, by and large, failed to rely on prayer and the power of God. We have drifted into a form of godliness without power (see 2 Tim. 3:5).

Unfortunately, many of us have often made the mistake of proceeding in our own efforts after only going through the motions of a few standard prayers, if any. Then we find ourselves living our lives and working in the ministry in our own strength. Reliance on self, rather than on the Holy Spirit, will always result in spiritual famine, for if we sow to the flesh, we will indeed reap the deeds of the flesh. If, however, we sow to the things of the Spirit, we will also reap in that area. (See Galatians 6:7-8.)

If we do the work of the ministry in our own strength, it may look like the favor of God is upon us for a season. We will see some fruitfulness from the use of our own natural giftings and talents. However, the consequences of spiritual famine and our own frustration will become increasingly evident over time.

Children's Minister, *please* don't be looking for new ways to entertain the children on Sunday mornings! Don't look in this book or that book for new "stuff" to use in Children's Church. Don't fill Sunday mornings with popcorn and videos. Yes, children are easily controlled and pacified when you put them in front of a video; but each time you do that, you are sacrificing the valuable training and ministry experience that you could be exposing them to.

I believe that the Lord is saying to every Children's Pastor exactly what He spoke to me. "I want to do something new. I want to do something different." Let's not cling to the old ways, to the familiar things. Let's respond with an enthusiastic, "Yes, Lord!" Let's allow God to do that new thing—in us and in our ministry.

You will be like a pioneer, going perhaps where no one has gone before. In every situation, ask the Holy Spirit to help you. Allow Him to do that new thing He wants to do in you and your ministry. And I encourage you to humble yourself to be able to learn from the little ones around you.

Chapter 5

The Children Still Lead

Then the word of the Lord came unto me, saying, Before I formed thee in the belly I knew thee; and before thou camest forth out of the womb I sanctified thee, and I ordained thee a prophet unto the nations. Then said I, Ah, Lord God! behold, I cannot speak: for I am a child. But the Lord said unto me, Say not, I am a child: for thou shalt go to all that I shall send thee, and whatsoever I command thee thou shalt speak (Jeremiah 1:4-7).

The call of God is upon our children. I believe it is important to place young boys and girls in roles of responsibility. I believe that we must release them to function now, not just "someday," in what God has called them to do.

Please understand that I am not suggesting that you, as an adult, neglect your God-given position of authority. You are to still be a leader. You are to set godly moral standards for children; you are to be an example of living according to those standards. You are to, prayerfully, line upon line and precept upon precept, lay foundations in the hearts of children so that as they continue to grow, their lives will be settled and strong.

> *Therefore whosoever heareth these sayings of Mine, and doeth them, I will liken him unto a wise man, which built his house upon a rock* (Matthew 7:24).

As the firm foundation of a relationship with God is laid in their lives, children will enter in with freedom and authority to the supernatural moving of His Spirit. We are called, not to teach cute little Bible lessons, but to preach the Word of God. Romans 10:17 says that faith comes by hearing the Word of God. If you want a group of boys and girls with hearts full of faith, teach them the Word. Then help them to not only hear it, but also put it into practice in their everyday lives. Teach them how to *do* God's Word.

A few weeks ago an unsaved family visited our church as the result of being invited by friends. Their six-year-old daughter, Spencer, came to Kingdom Kids. She went forward for prayer during the personal ministry time and was touched by the power of God. When her parents came to pick her up, Spencer was still lying peacefully on the floor. Neither parent seemed concerned about this. They simply waited patiently until Spencer got up and then they went home.

Spencer's father had been having back problems. A few days after their visit to our church, they were sitting together at the table when he began saying how badly his back was hurting. Spencer stood to her feet and said, "Dad, I have the power of Jesus in me! I'm going to lay my hands on you, and you are going to be healed!" She went over to her father, laid her hands on him, and prayed. Immediately he felt relief in his back. That in itself is a wonderful testimony, but there's more. The following week Spencer's mother and father came to a Friday evening service specifically to give their lives to the Lord. They went forward at the altar call and were saved.

Little Spencer is yet another example of the children leading. As we teach them the Word and continue to challenge them to put it into practice, and as we allow them to be touched by the Holy Spirit, I believe that we will have many more such testimonies.

Children are like young, tender plants. Instead of setting them out in the cold, harsh world, they need to be in a cozy hothouse for a good length of time. I believe we need to give them the best possible environment in their early years—a safe, protected place for them to soak up nutrients and get strengthened for the days ahead. As parents and teachers, we are called to protect our children. Some people have told me that they think I am sheltering my children too much. I respond, "You're doggone right I'm sheltering them!" If I don't shelter, lead, and direct my children, they will find something or someone who will. I think parents need to do more sheltering and less turning loose.

On Wednesday evenings, we have mid-week club meetings for boys and girls in our old building across the street. It amazes me how some parents will say to me, "When church is over, just let my kid go. He can come over to the sanctuary and find me there." Brownsville at night is not a place to let children run free. We will not just turn children loose. Parents are required to come and get them.

We also shelter and protect children in the area of spiritual ministry. A number of adults have come to Children's Church requesting prayer. We allow the children to pray for members of our congregation whom we know personally, and for visiting Children's Ministers only as we feel good about the person, and for both groups only under our close supervision. There are so many strangers coming to our services. We do not want any undesirable spirit imparted to our children as a result of their laying hands on someone. (If you believe that a blessing from God can be transferred by the laying on of hands, then know that the reverse is also possible!)

We give strong leadership in the areas of prayer, worship, and spiritual manifestations. I tell the children as they come forward for prayer that we are not looking for outward manifestations, but for inward changes of heart. I explain that sometimes when the power of God touches us, our bodies might jerk or shake. We might even fall down. If we do or if we don't, it doesn't matter. What matters is that we truly experience God.

Our Sunday morning Kingdom Kids for ages 6 through 12 is not a typical Children's Church meeting. It is a place of training. We are not just teaching the children *about* God; they are *experiencing* Him. We are not teaching them *about* serving the Lord; they are learning *how* and are being given opportunities to *do* the work of the ministry. For the Wednesday evening clubs, we have dozens of adult volunteers leading the different classes. Sunday mornings are different.

"This is Children's Church," I say to the boys and girls. "You guys are the children. Who do you think should run Children's Church?"

"You!" they respond.

"No, that would make it Pastor Vann's church. If this is really Children's Church, who do you think should run it?"

With wide-eyed realization they respond, "Me."

"That's right, you! I'm the pastor in here, but who do you think does all the work?"

"The children!"

"Right again! We have a prayer team. Who do you think makes up the prayer team?"

"The children!"

"We have people called 'wall watchers' all around the room to make sure that the children are behaving. Who do you think the wall watchers are?"

"The children!"

I go on and on down through the list. The children get it. They understand what we are trying to do on Sunday morning, and they love it. They are so eager to get involved in ministry that it keeps me praying for new things for them to do. God is gradually raising up leadership for new areas. We are presently developing a drama team under the leadership of Angie Griffin. I have wanted a drama team for a long time. It is so wonderful and releasing to just trust God in these areas instead of struggling to make something happen. When it was the right time, He spoke to the right person and now it just flows.

No one under the age of eight is put onto a ministry team. The six-and seven-year-olds understand that their role right now is one of observation and learning. They are looking ahead with great anticipation to when they will turn eight. I encourage them to be faithful and obedient; God and I are watching them, and their turn will come.

As I stated earlier, I see my role mainly as that of a facilitator. I am to give the children opportunities to express the giftings and talents God has given them. I am to mentor and guide them in areas of ministry. We now have about 14 adult volunteers who work with us on Sunday mornings on a regular basis in a variety of oversight capacities, but they really have very little to do. It is the children who actually do the work of the ministry. In the following pages I will try to give you a practical overview of some areas of ministry, and how we train and prepare the children on a weekly basis.

Prayer Team

In this, as well as every aspect of ministry, we are looking more for godly character and leadership qualities than for actual skill. Skill will come with training and experience. The children on prayer teams must meet high standards in their walk with Jesus. We are very careful whom we allow to lay hands on and minister to other children. We do not let a rebellious, disobedient child be part of the prayer team. I don't want that kind of spirit to be imparted to the other children!

Our prayer team is made up of eight- through twelve-year-olds. They wear little purple badges like the adult prayer team who serves in the sanctuary. Presently, there are 75 children on the team, and they minister on a rotating basis. A team of seven children minister each week. The group prays in a kind of buddy system, in three groups of twos. The seventh child is what we call the "comfort attender." This person carries an armload of cloths around and gently covers any children who fall under the power of the Spirit when they are prayed for. It brings a sense of security to the child on the floor. They feel it's okay to go ahead and rest in God's presence, to go ahead and give God time to do His work in their hearts. Covering them also allows for modesty.

Before the service each Sunday morning, the prayer teams meet for instruction and prayer. We tell them to simply allow themselves to be used by God. They aren't the ones who heal or answer prayer. God does that.

We use the same basic guidelines in choosing and training our prayer teams as are used with the adult prayer team in the sanctuary. We instruct the children as to what to pray and how to pray. They are limited to just a few words that they can pray, like, "More, Lord." They are to very gently lay their hands on the children's heads and they must never push a child when they are praying for them.

Worship Band

Kingdom Kids has a very dynamic worship team. This is one area where we involve mainly young teenagers rather than children because of the necessary skills required. The musicians in our band range in age from 12 to 16. They play keyboard, drums, bass, and guitar. The worship team rehearses for about two and a half hours on Saturday evenings. We use some "kids" songs and a lot of the "adult" songs from the sanctuary. (Chapter 9 is devoted entirely to worship, and I will share more details about the band then.)

Singers

Three of the older girls from the band sing on the lead microphones each week. We have found them to be stronger singers and better able to give leadership than the younger children. There are 44 young back-up singers who rotate on a weekly basis.

A few children on the team can't carry a tune in a tin bucket, but they are up there singing with all their hearts. That is the song God hears. I don't think He pays much attention to the quality of their voices; He is blessed by their hands raised to Him and by the way they inspire the other children to worship. We don't pay much attention to the quality of their voices either—we simply use discernment on the mixing board so that we, too, can enjoy the true song that's coming from their hearts. They can still hear themselves loud and clear through their monitor.

The singers rehearse for about two and a half hours on Saturday evenings with the band.

Wall Watchers

I use 11-and-12 year-olds for this ministry. This, too, is an area where we demand high standards. We speak to these children and tell them that we expect them to sit quietly and behave reverently. They are not allowed to talk to one another. They are not allowed to show any kind of favoritism when they each choose the child in their section who will receive that week's "quiet seat prize."

"The other children are watching you," I explain. "How can you expect them to behave if you don't? You are leaders and we expect you to show leadership qualities."

We have the boys sit on one side of the room and girls on the other. Each wall watcher has four rows of about nine children to oversee. Their primary responsibility is to help children implement the "Can Do Program." We have a list of all the things children "can do" in Children's Church. This list includes:

- You CAN sit up straight and tall.
- You CAN keep your hands to yourself.
- You CAN keep you feet on, or as close to, the floor as possible.
- You CAN sing out loud when it's time to sing out loud and sit real quiet when it's time to sit real quiet.
- You CAN talk *if* you have *the* microphone. (I used to say if you have *a* microphone. One ingenious little guy brought his own microphone into Children's Church!)

Some people have asked how we handle practical areas like bathroom breaks because of having such a large number of children for such a long time. We have very few children who need to use the bathroom during Children's Church because *everyone* goes around 10 o'clock. This takes about 15 minutes; then there is little disturbance throughout the rest of the meeting. (Note: Because our services last up to four hours, this 15-minute span is a valid investment of time. It may not be a good idea in other church settings if there is less time and fewer children.)

Puppet Team

The puppeteers are boys and girls who range in age from 10 to 12 years. They rehearse every Saturday evening from 5:00 to 6:30 p.m. with their adult leader, Rita Steeger. When Rita is not able to be there, her assistant, my 13-year-old daughter, Molly, takes the lead. We have about 25 puppeteers.

Our puppet ministry is not fun and games; it is ministry. Being on the puppet team takes commitment. Each child signs a statement saying they will pray and spend time in the Word on a daily basis. They agree to follow the clearly defined rules we give them regarding the handling of the puppets. The parents of the children also sign the paper, saying they will support their child's commitment. This includes bringing their child *on time* to the weekly rehearsals. If children are absent for three rehearsals, they are no longer on the puppet team.

I have one member on the team who has no lip synchronization abilities at all. This child opens the puppet's mouth when the song starts and closes it sometime before the song ends. I call this "ventriloquist puppetry." The puppet can talk but you don't see its mouth move. No problem. This child has a real heart to minister. As time passes, these skills will improve. I have several children who have been on the team for a year or two; they help train the new children.

We use the puppets to sing a special song during the offering or a slow worship song before the altar call, or possibly a wild crazy song as an opening. Puppets also show up regularly to teach memory verses. (They usually get the verses messed up and need the children to help them.)

Sound & Media Team

During both the puppet team and worship team rehearsals on Saturday evenings, the sound and camera people are in training. The sound team is learning how to run the board, set up microphones, etc. The camera crew actually films the rehearsals so as to gain more experience. One boy who runs cameras is Steve Hill's nine-year-old son, Ryan. These are not little camcorders I'm talking about. These are full configuration studio cameras.

Jason Bloodworth was one of the 11-and 12-year-olds I mentioned in an earlier chapter who began to line up at my door asking if there was something they could do when I first came to Brownsville. Jason liked playing around in technical areas. I asked an audio guy to come in and run the cables of our antique sound system to the back of the room. (It used to be tucked in behind the stage where we'd set it up—in hope that the volume would be consistent for the whole meeting.)

We found an old riser and a small platform hidden in a closet somewhere. On top, we set up a folding table, put the sound system on top of it, stuck Jason up there on a chair, and called him our sound man. That is exactly what Jason has become. Before we knew it, Jason was also running sound for youth meetings and helping in the sanctuary. Now, at the age of 16, Jason is hired by the church to run sound for the weekly morning teaching sessions and other meetings.

During this time, Jason got interested about the church's TV equipment. He started learning how to run a switcher and how to run cameras. Little did we know what Jason would be accomplishing in just a few short years. Now he is directing the filming of our Children's Church and training younger boys to do what he's doing.

Another young man, James Schleich, became interested in the sound equipment. He started asking a barrage of questions and reading every sound manual he could get his hands on. James is now 14 years old and he just finished writing a training booklet. He's called it "The Children's Church Audio Manual."

Greeters and Ushers

When boys and girls come in on Sunday mornings, they are greeted at the door and instructed to go to the tables at the back of the room where they sign in and pick up their name tags. Visiting children fill out a registration form and receive a gift bag. The tables are usually run by eight-year-olds, because all that is needed for this ministry is a friendly smile and an ability to read and write. I have different children involved each week. Another area where I use a variety of children is that of taking up the offering.

Servants

Every Saturday evening you will find a group of 15 to 20 children preparing our room for Sunday morning. They set up the name tags and the sign-in sheets and fill the visitor gift bags. They run vacuum cleaners and set up the chairs. My boys and girls know that I am somewhat of a perfectionist and if the chairs are out of line, they'll have to go back and straighten them. I've heard them saying things to each other like, "Pastor Vann won't put up with that!" And they're checking things out, making sure everything is just right.

On a recent Saturday evening, I walked in and saw one little girl with rubber gloves on. I asked her what she was doing. She answered me with a happy smile, "Cleaning the bathroom." Sure enough, she and another little girl scrubbed that washroom until it sparkled. I think the floor got washed three or four times that night. It is so beautiful to see the children taking responsibility and ownership like that.

Every week we have communion in Children's Church. What better place to gain an understanding of what Jesus did for us! What better place to remember His sacrifice on a weekly basis! Every week, children fill the cups and prepare the communion table. We could fill the communion cups in eight seconds with the machine in the church's communion room. Instead, we allow a couple of children to take about 15 minutes to fill the tray. They also fill the inside of the communion tray and various places around it. No problem. We just teach them how to clean up the mess.

Children also pass out the communion cups and bread. To be chosen to do that is a special honor.

But be ye doers of the word, and not hearers only, deceiving your own selves (James 1:22).

Brownsville's children aren't going to be like I was; they aren't going to have the same position that I had in the church as a child—the position of sitting still and being quiet. I heard the Word but I sat in a chair in Sunday school; I sat in a pew in church—week after week after week—doing nothing about the Word I was hearing. As a result, there was no anchoring of the Truth in my heart. Brownsville's children aren't going to be like I was and just hang around church without really knowing God. They are going to know Him and the joy of serving Him. They will know the joy of being anointed ministers.

These boys and girls are going to grow in the abilities God has given them. For the first time in their lives, someone is using them in ministry, and I believe that, as a result, they will continue to be in ministry for the rest of their lives. Brownsville's children aren't in church just because their Moms and Dads make them. They come because they have purpose; they are needed and they know it.

The little members of our church are seeing that there are many things they can do in the Body of Christ, and they are eating it up. They are learning wonderful life skills by working as teams. A wide variety of interpersonal relationship problems arise, especially during rehearsals. Each situation is just another chance for learning! What better way for children to learn about communication and conflict-solving! Many of us wish we had had a similar opportunity instead of having to learn to deal with people issues as adults.

It is time that we as parents, pastors, and Children's Ministers begin to realize that God's children can be powerful earth shakers and movers if they are taught God's truths, trained in the use of spiritual gifts, and released to *do* what they have learned.

I am looking with great anticipation toward the future. What benefits we will reap from providing the children with opportunities to discover and nurture their God-given talents and abilities! In a very few years we will not have to go outside the church to find spiritually mature, trained, and experienced people in any area of ministry. A group of committed, solid young ministers will be standing before us saying, "Here am I. Send me."

Chapter 6

A Typical Week With Brownsville's Children

For in Him we live, and move, and have our being...
(Acts 17:28).

When revival hit, the Children's Ministry was greatly affected. It was non-stop church. People from across the nation and then from around the world began pouring to Brownsville. I tried to get help. I contacted a few other churches where God was moving and asked for their advice. One church said they had tried everything and now they did nothing. They didn't even offer nursery for their ministry teams. I knew that in our setting, I needed to come up with something. In this chapter, I will outline for you what we are presently doing to provide nurturing care and training for children on a weekly basis.

Nursery

Sandra Bloodworth works at our church fulltime as the Children's Ministry secretary and Nursery Director. She is a gift from God to this church and to this revival; her heart is dedicated to the nurturing care of our littlest ones. Her goal is for every child, as he or she leaves the nursery, to leave with a feeling of having been loved.

Many children spend their days in day-care settings. Although the facilities we offer are similar to those of day care, Sandra's desire is for the children to be aware of a difference at church; to have an extra sense of being loved and cared for; to feel, in fact, the presence of the Lord.

Every experience that a child has is a learning experience. They learn either positive or negative things, but they are learning. Sandra teaches her workers to watch for opportunities to instill godly principles into the lives of the children. If a child falls in one of the nurseries and gets a "boo-boo," the worker's *first response* must be to pray for that child, and then to go for the Band-Aid or the ice pack that may be needed. As a result, children will learn that the first thing to do when they are in some kind of trouble is to pray! They will learn to take their cares to the Lord.

By the time a child is five years of age, the way he or she will respond to life situations has already been set in place. People who work in church nurseries have the awesome opportunity to establish a love for the Lord, a heart for His Word, and an excitement about church that will be foundational for a lifetime.

All our nursery workers receive training and encouragement. On Sunday mornings, each of our eight nurseries are manned by one paid professional plus adult volunteer members of our congregation. Our policy is that no one under the age of 18 is allowed to work in the nurseries. This is primarily for liability reasons. People who have children in the nursery and who have been in our church for longer than six months are automatically put on a volunteer schedule. If the time they have been assigned is inconvenient, they are responsible to switch dates with someone else and contact Sandra regarding the change.

For the evening revival services, we hire nursery workers to care for children from infancy up to five years of age. If we were dependent on volunteers for the evening services, we would need 275 people on a rotating basis. The logistics of this are mind-boggling, particularly when our revival services can last for eight hours. Most people are not used to being in a room full of tiny people for that length of time. (I didn't want any of our people going around bald because they pulled their hair out!)

We presently hire 34 nursery workers. They are carefully screened and interviewed to ensure their Christian commitment and life standards. A large number of these people are day care professionals; some are students in our School of Ministry. These 34 workers are rotated, and we have about 24 people a night working the eight nurseries. We follow Florida state guidelines regarding the number of workers needed in proportion to the number of children. When a nursery reaches the allowed number of children on any given evening, that nursery is closed. This is done for safety reasons. We feel that this is our responsibility—to follow the state laws and to maintain a safe, loving environment for the children. Each nursery has a camera that constantly scans the room, monitoring and recording what is happening.

Our nursery services have structured teaching, worship, and free playtime. We use a good, basic foundational curriculum for the two-, three-, four-, and five-year-olds. Quiet Christian music is played in all of the nurseries, and each child is prayed for.

In her welcoming letter in the front of our nursery manual, Sandra says, "If you are ready to meet needs, encourage parents, and be instrumental in molding behavior and developing attitudes which will become a life-long part of children's lives, then let's get started!"

Mid-Week Clubs

For the first three months of the revival, all mid-week programs in every area of church life were canceled. It took us that long to realize that God planned to stay. (We thought He had just come to visit.) At the beginning, we took one day at a time, then one week at a time. Steve Hill kept clearing his calendar to stay a little longer; then he and his family just moved to Pensacola.

Gradually we went back to some normal weekly functions, although our church will never again be "normal." Everything we do now has a revival touch to it—no more dead, lifeless programs. We are doing our best to try to hear God, and only institute *His* programs. Pastor John has done a wonderful job of meeting the needs of the flock in the midst of opening the doors of our church to thousands of visitors each week.

The only mid-week children's meetings we have are "Royal Rangers" for the boys and "Missionettes" for the girls. About 350 children meet on Wednesday nights from 7:00 until 8:30 p.m. These programs are offered through the Assemblies of God. The boys and girls love the Bible memorization, awards, and activities.

Dana gives oversight to the Missionette program, and Fred Geer oversees the Royal Rangers. We have no problem getting workers for Wednesday nights. The programs are very successful, and people are simply drawn to volunteer.

They are from every walk of life and of a wide age span. The people who teach those classes make a year-long commitment. They know that is where God wants them. As a result, the whole program is a joy—for them, for the children, and for Fred, Dana, and I!

Sunday Morning Ministry

One hour before the main service each week, we offer Sunday school classes for every age group. Our goal is to provide foundational Bible teaching for the children so that they will have a working knowledge of the Scriptures by the time they complete the elementary school level. In recent years in the Church, there has been a strong turning toward Children's Church and away from Sunday school. I feel that children need both. Just like adults, youngsters need small group catechism-style teaching as well as the corporate excitement of creative preaching.

I have heard people say things like, "We need to stop teaching the Bible stories. Kids get sick of hearing about Noah over and over again. They've been listening to David and Goliath for years and years!" My response is that *children haven't been around for years and years!* The stories are new to young children, and they need to learn the foundational principles that those stories teach. We must, however, be careful not to present the same stories to each age group. There must be a systematic strategy so that the children come away with a solid understanding of God's Word. We must make a conscious plan to teach not only Bible stories, but also the Scriptures. Paul said to Timothy that "from a child you have known the holy Scriptures," *not* "from a child you have known the Bible stories" (see 2 Tim. 3:15). Children need to know their Bible verses—how to look up verses and how to apply God's Word to their daily lives.

In order to accomplish this, we draw from a wide variety of resources and curriculum, and we are very blessed to have excellent teachers. The people who serve in this area make a one-year commitment to their specific age group. We have many people who teach year after year after year. They know the value of what they are doing. They know the value of sound, systematic teaching in the lives of boys and girls.

Following the Sunday school classes, our Kingdom Kids meeting runs throughout the entire adult service, which can be up to four hours in length. Our Children's Church is truly a **Children's** *Church*. Although about 14 adult volunteers serve in a variety of oversight capacities, the actual ministry is done almost entirely by children. The Kingdom Kids do the work, I preach, and some adult volunteers stand in the back to pray and keep watch.

People ask me, "But how can you keep more than 300 children for four hours?" I can't; God can. Pastor John says that I am the only Children's Pastor he's ever known who would tell him, "*We've GOT to have four hours! Please don't cut us short today!*" Many times if parents come to pick up their boys and girls after three and a half hours, we aren't done yet. They will find their children on the altars. They will find their children prostrated on the floor. I've had parents come and sit in awe, watching their A.D.D. (Attention Deficit Disorder) child who has been lying on the floor for the past 30 minutes under the power of the Spirit.

One of the main questions that I am asked by visiting Children's Ministers is regarding what curriculum I use. I have tried many curriculums and have been more than a little disappointed with the majority of them. Much of what is available is primarily geared toward entertaining children. Our boys and girls here at Brownsville have tasted the Spirit. They don't want to be entertained.

Now, don't get me wrong. We have fun on Sunday mornings. We start off with wild crazy songs. We keep things upbeat and moving. We try to keep the lessons interesting. But the goal of everything we do is to have the children experience the presence and reality of God. It is only in His presence that they will really have fun and be satisfied.

I like using a 13-week quarterly style of curriculum because it helps me stay on track. I like to build from one meeting to the following one. I don't want Mary and Joseph going to Jerusalem one week and King Saul hunting for David the next! It is important to lay truth in children's lives in a methodical way. As Isaiah 28:10 says, "precept upon precept, line upon line." Because I believe this so strongly, and because of the multitude of creative teaching ideas that the Holy Spirit has been releasing in our ministry, we are presently writing such a curriculum, which will be available for purchase.

Whatever curriculum or plan you use, the most important factor is being open to the Holy Spirit. Be prepared. Pick and choose from a variety of sources to help you say what you feel God wants you to say. Have your plan and materials ready, but don't cling to them. Allow God to prompt you and be sensitive to how the children are responding. You may need to belabor some point, to skip another, or to add something you had never thought of. This freedom, however, can only come as you are ready. Never walk into a children's meeting without a plan. Never attempt to minister without having prayed and prepared for that meeting. The children will tear you apart.

I generally use Tuesdays to plan the following Sunday morning children's meeting. This gives me time to meditate on the theme and to acquire any necessary items I might need for the object lessons. I love object lessons, by the way. They are my favorite way to teach children. Object lessons are wonderful tools to demonstrate intangible principles in a tangible way. Children can relate to visual illustrations. Another reason I enjoy using object lessons is that God gives them to me. They are Holy Spirit inspired, and I find it easy to receive this kind of inspiration. Everyone who teaches children must find the method that comes most naturally to them. God will quicken your gifts and abilities so that what you impart to the children will be fresh and life-giving.

Every week, I have a list of 15 different elements I would like to include in the service. From beginning to end, each element flows along one central theme. My list includes things like the Bible lesson, memory verse, object lessons, puppets, and a variety of kinds of songs. I have my one central theme broken up into "bite sized" portions for the children.

Recently, I have been very blessed to have some of the students from the Brownsville School of Ministry desire to learn about Children's Ministry. Our School of Ministry started in January of 1996 with 156 students. In less than one year it grew to 576 students.

Matthew Oliver is one of the students who has come alongside and is working with us in Children's Ministry. God has been giving Matthew some wonderfully creative teachings. One week I asked him to tell the story of

Potiphar's wife from Genesis 39. Now, this is a difficult portion of Scripture to teach children! Well, Matthew came up with an illustration of "the king's cookie jar." He told how no one was supposed to eat out of the king's cookie jar. Potiphar's wife had Joseph arrested for eating cookies out of the king's cookie jar, but she was the one with crumbs all over her face. At the end of his wildly animated story, Matthew said, "This is not exactly how the story goes in the Bible. You'll have to read it for yourself." The children loved it. So did I.

We usually begin the morning with some wild, crazy song, but we do most of our singing later in the service. I try to get through the preliminary elements before I reach worship, because more and more often, we get stuck there and never get back to any teaching. (It's wonderful! More on this is in a later chapter.)

We are having so much fun being prepared—to let the Holy Spirit take control. We are prepared—to get out of the Holy Spirit's way and let Him do what He wants. One Friday night, two little girls who were sisters came to me and said, "Pastor Vann, we've been working on an interpretive dance. Can we do it on Sunday at Children's Church?" Now, I had my theme, and I don't want to just put any dance or song into a service unless it flows. I asked them what the song was. " 'Marching and Moving' " by Carmen, they responded.

I was unfamiliar with the title, so I told the girls to bring the words in on Sunday morning, and I would let them do their dance some week when it would fit into the meeting. That was on a Friday night. The next day I was pulling final things together for Sunday morning. I wanted to add a video clip, so I scanned our shelves for something that would fit with that week's theme, "Raising the Standard." A Carmen video stood out to me. There were the words to "Marching and Moving." The song was a perfect fit with what I wanted to say at that point of the service!

I quickly called the girls. Their dad answered the phone and told me his daughters were out playing with a neighbor. I asked him to let the girls know that, yes, they could minister the next morning. The dad was surprised. "I've been watching them dance to that song around here for weeks. You let the kids do stuff like that?" he asked. I told him that we not only let them, we also encourage them to minister in the areas of their giftings. He said, "I'm going to have to come and see this!"

Those little girls worked for two extra hours Saturday evening, polishing and perfecting their dance. What they did the next morning was not a performance. It was God-ordained ministry. Dad and Mom stood grinning from ear to ear watching their little daughters dance before the Lord. I love it when God puts a service together.

Since that time, more children have come up to me wanting to minister in some creative area. I tell them to try to bring the song or whatever it is to me before Friday night in case I need it that Sunday! I have been finding more and more how God is giving the children things to do that fit exactly with my next theme. I encourage the children over and over that we do not want performances. We don't want boys and girls showing off for an audience. We want them to do their dance or song for Jesus, with a heart of worship to Him.

We don't want performances; we want reality. Our goal is for everything that happens on Sunday mornings to have a touch of God on it. I don't want to settle for mediocrity. I am aiming for excellence. We must teach children to strive and reach out for God in every area of their lives.

A Typical Week With Brownsville's Children's Pastor

I want to conclude this chapter by talking to you about how our personal life goes on a weekly basis. This is yet another commonly asked question. People want to know how we survive revival. How do we balance family life while being at church almost every day for two-and-a-half years? How does Dana manage to do all that she does—and home school our children on top of it all?

When revival first hit, it was all we could do to hold on. The thing took off so fast that we felt like all we were doing was hanging on and trying not to fall off (or, in my case, trying not to *jump* off!). But now things have settled. The Lord is training us so that we are able to keep going for the long haul. We don't feel like we are struggling now to keep our heads above water. We learned to float. Now we aren't trying to carry the revival; the revival is carrying us. We don't feel tired. We're not burned out. The River is carrying us.

My family has been transformed by revival. There really is no such thing as spare time in our lives. We used to pray and ask God to be involved in our busy schedules. Now we are involved in *His*! The long list of activities that we once held dear has been exposed for what it is: emptiness. Gone are all the frivolous things that ate up our time but had no eternal value. One of our most popular yet grammatically poor sayings is, "*It just don't matter anymore.*" What matters to us now is seeing hundreds of people running to the altar night after night. What matters to us now is that God is moving mightily by His Spirit, and we are so blessed and honored as a family to be right in the middle of one of the places where He is sending revival.

My typical week begins by taking Mondays off. There are no services Sunday or Monday nights. I am at the church Tuesday through Sunday. I generally go in around 9:00 a.m. and stay until midnight or 1:00 that night. On occasion, Dana will get a little concerned that I haven't been home. It does get a little funny sometimes. I can imagine people on the outside watching our driveway. I come in at 4:00 p.m. I take a shower, eat, and at 5:00 p.m. I'm going back out in a suit. I return at 1:00 a.m. and go back out at 9:00 a.m. Back and forth; in and out; over and over.

"But isn't that a tremendous sacrifice?" people ask. My answer is "yes." Yes, it is a sacrifice. The whole family sacrifices. Our entire church family sacrifices. An average of 350 people volunteer for every revival service. I watch dedicated men and women who night after night after night come out to serve in some area of ministry after putting in 8 or 10 hours at their regular jobs. I watch retired people put in 60 hours a week at church.

On many revival nights, the Children's Church area (cafeteria) is used as an extra seating area. People come in who have spent from 8 to 12 hours standing in line, and now they find themselves in an overflow area with a large screen hook-up to the sanctuary. Those people need somebody to love on them a little bit. They are hot and sweaty and tired and disappointed to be in an overflow area. (Actually, many people have said they feel a very powerful anointing there in the cafeteria. We think it could be because it has been used as our pre-service intercessory prayer room for many years. And, of course, it is also where Children's Church is held!)

Anyway, to help people relax and feel loved a little bit, I generally have a time of questions and answers. They usually ask why I think God picked Brownsville. I say how I am at church at least 60 hours each week; how I feel extremely blessed to be able to serve the Lord and His people and get paid for it.

Then I pull one of the ushers over, put an arm around his shoulders, and say, "This guy is here 60 hours every week, too. But he doesn't get paid for it. Why did God choose Brownsville? Because of the hundreds of people like him."

Revival costs everything. I believe that God knew this was a church where the pastor and the people would pay the price. Pastor John was desperate for a move of the Holy Spirit. He tells the story of how he prayed and asked God to put him where He was going to send revival. Pastor John didn't care if that meant he would end up in little tiny church of 50 people. He didn't care; he wanted revival at any cost. The people picked up Pastor's heart cry and paid the price in prayer long before we saw the Holy Spirit move. God saw Pastor's heart and He saw the servant heart of the people here. He saw that the people were willing to make the necessary sacrifices and changes just to be whatever God wanted us to be.

The Destiny Image *Digest*, a quarterly magazine publication, recently devoted an entire issue to this revival (Vol. 5, No. 1). To help you understand the magnitude of what is happening here at Brownsville, I want to give the following quotations from that magazine (and please note that these statistics are constantly rising):

"What would you do if 1,552,000 people came to your services?

"Your toilet paper and cleaning supplies have to be dropped off weekly in large trucks, along with a bill topping $2,000 a month! Your water bill might help finance the next water plant expansion. Your altar worker list fills almost six single-spaced pages.... You may well be the only church in town where 'rent-a-cops' show up for duty in your parking lots almost every night of the week to handle security and parking.

"Somehow your secretarial and administrative staff have learned how to deal with the hundreds of calls a day from nearly every continent that bombard eight overworked incoming phone lines. Your electrical bill comes in an overstuffed envelope because you have been lighting and cooling most of your main buildings for 18 to 24 hours a day, five and six days a week....

"Your pastoral staff often 'makes do' on three or four hours of sleep a day, because they work with scores of prayer teams to lay hands upon and pray for nearly 3,000 people each service, followed by an army of assistants who try to 'catch' the majority of people who fall under the anointing during the whirlwind of ministry. Yet everyone is still smiling.

"What is going on? *Revival.*"

Our typical week is simply what we feel a typical, normal Christian's week *should* look like. Revival life usually appears to be extremely radical for those who are not yet walking in it. However, it is not at all radical according to the standards of God's Word. He is simply bringing us back to the purpose for which we were created—to live and move and have our very being in Him.

Part 3

Children of Revival

Chapter 7

Shaking, Quaking, or Faking?

Then I heard him speaking, and as I listened to him, I fell into a deep sleep, my face to the ground. A hand touched me and set me trembling on my hands and knees (Daniel 10:9-10 NIV).

Manifestations. Noah Webster's 1828 dictionary gives this definition: "The act of disclosing what is secret, unseen, or obscure; discovery to the eye or to the understanding the exhibition of any thing by clear evidence."

Somehow, mostly through the critical voices of people who have never even witnessed the "manifestations" at Brownsville, the *word manifestation* has taken on a freakish, mystical feeling when in, fact it, means just the opposite. To make something manifest means to make it plain and obvious!

In these days, God's presence in people's lives has been made plain and obvious. When the supernatural touch of God comes upon our natural bodies, His power is manifested—it is made clearly evident. When we stop to think about *God* the Creator of the universe, the One who holds up everything by the Word of His power—actually touching a person...it is mind-boggling! And the fact that our bodies shake or quiver or fall down *should* surprise us! We should be surprised that we *lived through it*!

Many people who have been touched by the powerful outpouring of God's Spirit in the earth today have a renewed interest in Church history. Through their study they are seeing parallels in what God is doing now and what He has done many times throughout Church history. People are also seeing similarities in the many areas across the world where churches are experiencing revival. These similarities are almost like a "Welcome Home" sign to visitors from other revival centers.

Let me say very clearly that our attention is not on the manifestations themselves. Our attention is on changed lives. During the past two and a half years we have seen people respond to the touch of God's power in a multitude of ways. Over and over and over again the result of that kind of encounter with God has been exactly what we have looked for—changed lives. People are simply not the same as they used to be. The changes vary from folks simply having a greater hunger for God to people who have received supernatural, divine healings. We have seen thousands of first time conversions plus thousands of re-dedications to the Lord. We have seen families restored, rebellious children turned into on-fire Christians, and worn-out ministers refreshed and renewed.

What a shame that some people have chosen to disregard what God has been doing just because they don't understand it.

Likewise the Spirit also helpeth our infirmities: for we know not what we should pray for as we ought: but the Spirit maketh intercession for us with groanings which cannot be uttered (Romans 8:26).

In Brownsville, the greatest area in which we see "manifestations" is that of intercession. God wants us to feel His feelings. When He shares with us through the revelation of the Holy Spirit, we get a little taste of His heart for the lost. He is not willing that any should perish (see 2 Pet. 3:9). He longs for people to turn from their wicked ways (see Is. 55:7). He is the Father—yearning for the prodigals to come home (see Lk. 15:11-24). Sometimes the burden to pray and weep comes upon His people so strongly that it would be almost impossible not to respond.

Ezekiel 22:29-31 speaks of how God is looking for someone to "stand in the gap." Standing in the gap means to stand between the judgment of God and the person who is on his or her way to hell and destruction.

When you look around Brownsville Assembly during an altar call and see people weeping for the lost, crying out to God for His mercy toward sinners, you just can't help but understand that this is the way it should be. Souls are weighing in the balances.

Many times the weeping is accompanied by outward bodily movements. Sometimes it feels like God is crying through you. He is looking for willing, yielded vessels. In an earlier chapter, I told you about how one night our daughter,

Whitney, kept weeping and reaching down as if pulling souls out of hell.

One evening early on in the revival a little girl named Aimee began trembling and bowing at the waist. People sitting near Aimee knew that God was touching her in a miraculous way. They watched as she lifted her hands toward Heaven and began bending her knees and running on the spot. Her hands and arms were shaking quite dramatically.

After about 15 minutes of this consistent motion, which would be almost impossible to accomplish in the natural, the woman who was looking after Aimee leaned over and asked what was happening. A little out of breath, and continuing to keep her hands raised before the Lord, Aimee responded, "An angel is holding me up by the hands and shaking the sin out of me!"

One of the most frequently seen bodily movements is intercessory bowing. Some call this the prophetic spiritual birthing of souls. It is the most common form of intercession during the altar calls at Brownsville. The weight of what is best described as a glory blanket will begin pushing the person's head and shoulders down so that he or she bends at the waist. When this weightiness comes upon you, usually the only way to stop yourself from bending is to make a conscious choice to quit worshiping, or to quit praying for souls.

It is interesting to note that right before the altar call ends, most intercession stops. Sometimes the speaker will see this ceasing in intercession as confirmation that it is time to move on in the service.

I love watching children yield to the Spirit of God when He prompts them to pray. We have several children each week who spend the entire church service on their faces, weeping for God to have His way that morning. If you know children, you know that this must have a supernatural source. No child that I have ever seen could spend four hours weeping—and not for themselves, but for God to have His way. No child that I know could tremble and shake for several hours unless the power of God was touching that child. No child that I know could "fall under the power" and remain lying on the floor quietly for extended lengths of time unless God Himself was the power that caused that child to go down.

"But is everything that goes on really God?" you might ask.

No, not everything. Like all of us, the children are human. Sometimes their own zeal and enthusiasm might just take over. Sometimes, when they get prayed for, they might just fall down on their own accord. Listen, what a great problem to have—a few children who are so hungry for reality that they fake it! *What would we rather have them imitate?*

Let me tell you a delightful little story about four-year-old Zachary Brown. Zachary marched into the four-year-old nursery one time and announced that he was the preacher; he was Steve Hill. The nursery workers stood around, amused. This was going to be so cute.

Zachary began by pulling a small group of other four-year-olds aside and instructing them on how to be his prayer team. Then he asked the other children to line up so that he could pray for them. They all lined up. As Zachary moved down the line praying, every child fell to the floor.

(People call this a variety of things like "falling out" or "being slain in the Spirit" or, as I stated earlier, getting "zapped.") Now, you would expect those little children to jump right back up. They didn't. Many of them were powerfully touched by God. They lay there quietly on the floor for a good length of time. The nursery workers were going nuts!

Was this faking? You'll have to come to your own conclusions.

Occasionally I have seen a child imitating some kind of manifestation; he or she may shake or tremble or cry or lie down on the floor. Dana and I pray for discernment. Imitation is a valid form of childhood expression. Children learn through play and imagination. Most of us have seen young children "playing church." If a child is "playing church" and his church happens to be in revival, surely that child will imitate what he has seen. I see this as harmless. It is actually a very logical way for children to become comfortable with yielding to the Spirit of God, to help them be prepared when the true experience actually occurs.

If, however, we feel that the child is imitating some manifestation and is seeking to draw attention to himself, we go and speak to him or her. We teach the children and give them instruction. We tell them that anything they do is to be for the glory of God, never for the attention or approval of other people.

The same is true if we see a child supposedly "dancing in the Spirit." We have had many instances of children truly "dancing in the Spirit." It is absolutely beautiful to see them glide around the room as if they are dancing with the Lord.

I believe that is exactly what they are doing. Their eyes are closed, their hands are raised, and they move gracefully in and out and around people and furniture as if an unseen Hand is guiding them.

This is much different from simply dancing happily before the Lord. We encourage the children to clap and rejoice during worship. But if we see a child dancing as if in the Spirit and she is very conscious of her movements and is looking to see who is watching her, then we will confront that child. It is one thing to have a sincere hunger to worship the Lord; it is quite another to try to draw attention to yourself.

When we confront any child about manifestations, it is always in a gentle, teaching manner, never harshly. We seek to pastor and guide them in how to move with the Holy Spirit. If, for example, a child on the worship team begins to jerk or shake on the platform, we observe for a moment, asking the Lord for discernment and guidance. Sometimes we will move the child behind the puppet stage or to the back of the room where he or she can fully yield to the Holy Spirit without being a distraction to the other children.

We are very cautious about making sure that what happens in Children's Church is not something that is manufactured. I do not want children to experience a counterfeit. I want what they experience to be real.

A frequent criticism of manifestations goes something like this, "God is a gentleman. He will never force His will upon you. He will never *make* you do something you don't want to do." My response is, "*Really?!*"

I wonder what Saul of Taursus would say about that? Was God being a gentleman when He knocked him off his horse on the road to Damascus? Was God being a gentleman when He struck Saul with blindness? (See Acts 9:3-9.)

Let No One Deceive You is a book written by Dr. Michael Brown, the Dean of Brownsville's School of Ministry. It is available through Destiny Image Publishers, and I highly recommend that you get a copy. The scriptural, historical, and witty approach in giving explanation to manifestations and other revival phenomenon makes it an invaluable resource book. Each chapter contains an incredible amount of quotes from past revivalists, including Jonathan Edwards, Charles Finny, and John Wesley. Dr. Brown quotes dozens and dozens of Scriptures that I am sure many of us never stopped to really consider. Here is one example of what he has to say in Chapter Ten (1997, 157-158):

"Yes, the very burden of prayer can be overwhelming and exhausting, even to the point of writhing and groaning in agony, and it is not without merit that many have spoken of the *agonies* of intercession. I believe the prophets of Israel would have had no problem at all with many of the most common manifestations in revival, including shaking and prostrations, not to mention being *consumed* with the burden of the Lord or being *undone* through an encounter with Him. In fact, they might say to us, 'That's nothing! Did you ever read what happened to *me*?'

"Listen to Habakkuk the prophet describe his reaction to the revelation of the glory of God: 'I heard and my heart pounded, my lips quivered at the sound; decay crept into my bones, and my legs trembled' (Hab. 3:16a). What would the critics do with a testimony like that in a revival service today?

" 'Tell me, sir, what happened to you in the meeting last night?' "

" 'Well, I heard the Word of the Lord thundering in my ears, and I felt like my insides were ready to burst. My heart felt like it was about to pound out of my chest. Then, I felt something like decay creep into my bones and I started to shake and quake all over. In fact, even as I speak of it now, my insides are trembling.'

" 'That's not God!' cries the critic. 'That's an altered state of consciousness at best and a demonic spirit at worst. The Holy Spirit doesn't cause things like that!'

" 'Sorry,' says the prophet. 'It's written in the Word!' (Please don't try to argue that things like that only happened during Bible days—which, by the way, is about as historically accurate as saying that people only got saved during Bible days. Has human nature changed since the canon of Scripture was completed? Can an encounter with God through His Word no longer shake us up?)"

David Walters, whom I believe to be a modern day children's revivalist, is the author of another book I highly recommend. *Children Aflame* (1995) includes a collection of writings taken from John Wesley's journals specifically regarding children being touched by the power of God in the 1700's.[1] When we speak about children of revival, it is very interesting to look back in the pages of history and read about some such children. The following are a few quotes from Wesley's journals as printed in David's book.

---

1. It is available through Good News Publishing, 220 Sleepy Creek Rd., Macon, Georgia 31210.

"**8/4/1755. (Death at Hayfield of a little girl)** She spoke exceedingly plain, yet very seldom; and then only a few words. She was scarce ever seen to laugh, or heard to utter a light or trifling word: she could not bear any that did, or behaved in a light or unserious manner...If her brothers or sisters spoke angrily to each other, or behaved triflingly, she either sharply reproved, (when that seemed needful) or tenderly entreated them to give over. If she spoke too harshly to any, she would humble herself to them, and not rest until they had forgiven her. After her health declined she was particularly pleased with hearing that hymn sung, 'Abba Father' and would be frequently singing that line to herself, 'Abba Father, hear me cry.'

"On Monday April the 7th, without any struggle, she fell asleep, having lived **two years and six months.**"

(Note: In the 1700's many children died through plagues and diseases.)

"**30/7/1758. (Cork)**" I began meeting with the **children** in the afternoon, though with little hopes of doing them good; but I had not spoken long on our natural state before many of them were in tears, and five or six so affected, that they could not refrain from crying aloud to God. When I began praying, their cries increased, so that my voice was soon lost."

24/5/1759. (Thursday) ...fifteen or sixteen persons felt the arrows of the Lord, and dropped down. A few of these cried out with the utmost violence, and little intermission, for some hours, but continued struggling, as in the pangs of death. I observed, besides these, one **little girl** deeply convinced, and a **boy, nine or ten years old**. Both these, and several others, when carried into the parsonage-house, either lay as dead, or struggled with all their might: but in short time, their cries increased beyond measure, so that the loudest singing could scarce be heard. Some at last called on me to pray, which I did, and for a time, all were calm: but the storm soon began a again. Mr. Hicks then prayed and afterward Mr. Berridge: but still, though some received consolation, others remained in deep sorrow of heart."

People have accused manifestations as being a result of emotionalism or moving in the flesh. I'd like you to take a moment to consider something. Which emotion toward God is better—zealousness or blind apathy? What is more soulish and fleshly—yielding to the Holy Spirit when He wants to touch your life or digging in your heels and refusing to give up your right to control?

Can we resist when God is trying to touch us? Yes, in many instances, I believe we can. But we here at Brownsville don't want to. We want to allow Him complete freedom. We want to give up our right to control and say one of the favorite phrases around here, "More, Lord!"

Last summer, I took 50 children to a children's camp in another state. During the altar call on Monday night, some of our little girls began to intercede. They bowed low at the waist. They began to moan and weep, praying for the Lord to have His way at the camp and at that altar call. Gradually their weeping increased volume and they began to wail with the burden of the Lord.

The camp leader took me aside and said that kind of thing would not be allowed at their camp. He spoke to me about his concerns, voicing some of the typical criticisms such as God being a God of order etc. Because I myself had such a difficult time at the beginning of the revival, I could understand where he was coming from. I tried to explain what we had learned over the past few years; the changes we had seen in the lives of the children; some scriptural and historical ways God has touched people... He was still adamant. That kind of thing would not be allowed at their camp.

That night, I called Pastor John for advice. Should I just pack up the children and come home? He said we should try to stay. We were at their camp; we should submit to their rules. He told me to try to explain this to the children.

After I hung up, the Lord gave me a beautiful idea. Luke 19:40 says that if we don't praise the Lord, the rocks will cry out. I went to speak to my little intercessors. I picked up a rock and said, "We can't cry out here. Listen, if God wants you to cry out, and you can't, He'll have the rocks do it for you!" I tucked the rock into my pocket. The next thing I knew, those little girls all had rocks in their pockets. Whenever the burden came on them to pray, they squeezed their rocks real tight and held on.

Let me interject here two instances that happened on that first night. I was sharing with our bus driver how the little girls had interceded and he began to weep. "Pastor Vann, I am not right with the Lord." I was able to lead him in prayer.

Also that night, while I was on the camp pay phone with Dana, one of the chaperones who had traveled with us to camp sat on a bench waiting for me. Mike Steeger, the husband of our puppet team leader, Rita Steeger, noticed a teenage girl waiting to use the phone. Mike felt prompted by the Lord to go and speak to her. I watched from the phone booth as they talked. I saw Mike take her hands and I watched her cry as they prayed together.

This girl was a pastor's daughter. She had been walking in rebellion and her parents had sent her to work at the camp, hoping she would get her life turned around. That night she was planning to call her folks and tell them not only that she was leaving the camp, but also that she was running away and they would never see her again. Mike was able to minister to this girl. She opened her heart and shared her fears and struggles. She did get turned around at camp—that night. I believe that our little intercessors had a part to play in her life.

There were several particularly anointed speakers at camp. The altar call on Wednesday was very powerful and heart-touching. Our girls were biting their tongues and hanging on real tight to the rocks in their pockets. One or two of them got up and left the meeting with a counselor to try to get their breath.

Then the speaker asked all the workers to come up and pray for the children at the altar. I walked up and put my hands on two of our boys who were receiving prayer. The Spirit of God hit me. I had been able to stay pretty controlled up until that point. But now I suddenly bent at the waist and gave a loud moan. Uh-oh. I went to join the girls who were now all outside, struggling to keep from interceding. I put my arms around them, and we all wept. "The rocks will cry out for us, girls. God knows our hearts. He will have His way."

Later, Mike was out in the parking lot trying to gather a group of six boys who had come to camp from the inner city. They were actually more like a gang than a group. Those boys had been a problem all week—talking and acting ugly. Earlier that evening, some of the boys we had brought to camp came and complained to me about how this gang had been cussing and making some rude and obscene gestures. I asked my boys if they had prayed for them; they said that no, they hadn't. A few minutes later I saw about ten of our boys standing in a circle, praying.

When I looked over at the parking lot, there was Mike getting the "gang members" to all join hands as he led them to the Lord! The next morning, those boys were not the same boys. Something had happened to them. Everyone at camp noticed the dramatic change in their behavior. I believe that this was a direct answer to the prayers of our children.

After supper on the last night, some Children's Ministers who had brought children to camp were waiting on the dining hall porch to speak to us. One of them said, "I went back to my room on Monday night when your girls prayed like that and I didn't understand. Then the Holy Spirit spoke to me and said, 'I am doing this'. I firmly believe what you did was of God." Another man said, "When I was packing my clothes to come here to camp, the Holy Spirit spoke to me and told me to 'look up and see what I am about to do'. When those children began to intercede and cry out to God, I realized that this was what the Holy Spirit had been speaking about. I realized that God is doing some different things than what we are used to."

After our 50 children got settled in their seats on the bus that evening, I asked those leaders to share what they had told me with our children. One by one they took the bus microphone and did so. Then another one of the Children's Ministers asked if he could speak to our boys and girls. He climbed up the bus steps and stood at the front. "I just wanted to tell you guys that I've been watching you this week," he said. "You kids are different than the others I have seen here. You stand out as being different—different for God. I just wanted to thank you."

As he left, I pulled the rock out of my pocket, lifted it high and said, "The rocks have cried out!" Our 50 boys and girls stood up and cheered.

Let me stress yet again that what we are looking for is not manifestations themselves, but the visible outward signs of God at work in the lives of the children. There are children who will bow, shake, and jerk; others moan, weep, groan and wail loudly. I don't consider any of these things out of line. But I am not looking so much at what they do then, as at what they do *after* the experience. What has happened to the children themselves? What changes have occurred in their lifestyles?

Believe me, we have seen changes. We are seeing children who are walking in the anointing of God.

These children are like the living epistles Paul speaks of in Second Corinthians 3:2-3. They are walking examples of what God can and will do as we yield to Him with the humility of childlike faith. They are what I call living object lessons.

Chapter 8

Living Object Lessons

An object lesson is simply using something visible to explain a spiritual principle. I believe that object lessons are one of the most scriptural techniques for teaching. Throughout the Bible we see the use of symbolic illustrations—from Genesis to the Old Testament prophets; continually in the ministry of Jesus; and throughout the New Testament. Here are just a very few examples:

- Genesis 9:12-13—Rainbow as a visual symbol of promise
- 1 Kings 11:30-32—Torn garment
- Isaiah 64:8; Jeremiah 18:1-6—Potter and clay
- Jeremiah 24—Good and bad figs
- Matthew 6:28—Lilies of the field
- Matthew 5:13-16—Salt and light
- Acts 21:11—Agabus tying up Paul
- 2 Timothy 2:20-21—Different kinds of vessels

There are many, many prophetic symbols of Christ throughout Scripture—the sacrifice of lambs (Ex. 12:3-28); the rock (Ex. 17:6; Ps. 61; 62); the plumbline (Amos 7:7-8);

the bread (Mt. 26:26); the wine (Mk. 14:23-25); the High Priest (Zech. 6:12-13); and the tree of life (Rev. 22:2).

God uses things we can see to teach us about the Holy Spirit: water (Jn. 7:38-39); fire (Mt. 3:11); wind (Acts 2:2); oil (Ps. 45:7); rain and dew (Hos. 6:3); and the dove (Mt. 3:16)

When we instruct boys and girls in the things of God, instead of merely speaking words, we would do well to follow the scriptural example using objects and symbolism. I pray constantly for the Lord to give me a multitude of creative ideas to teach His ways to children.

During the altar call of every evening revival service, children ten years of age and under who have come forward to receive Jesus as their Savior are invited to spend a few minutes with Pastor Vann.

This gives me the opportunity to speak to them in a setting where there are fewer distractions. I want them to understand the commitment they have just made to Jesus. I begin by asking them why they went up to the altar. I go on to explain, saying the words of a prayer doesn't save anyone. The way to be saved is to believe in your heart and make a commitment to Jesus.

I talk to the children about having Jesus as their best friend. I go up to a few of them and shake their hands. "Hello. Will you be my best friend?" Each child invariably says that, yes, he or she will. Then I back away from them and say, "It's sure great to have you for my best friends; I hope I see you again someday." Then I walk back to the front of the room.

"Are we really best friends now?" I ask. Some of them nod and some of them shake their heads, confused. "How could we be best friends?" I ask. "I don't know where you are from. I don't know what kind of house you live in or what your favorite food is. I don't know what makes you sad, or what makes you happy. Best friends know stuff like that about each other!"

I go on and talk about how children, and adults, too, come to the Lord. They shake hands with Him and say, "Thank You, Jesus, for saving me. See ya later." Then they go right back out and live exactly like they used to live. They go right back to doing the things they want to do, and not what Jesus wants them to do. I say, "They are not best friends with Jesus, just like the boys and girls I shook hands with tonight are not best friends with me." Then we go on to talk about how you become best friends with God.

For years I have felt that the Church has misled people of every age by saying that all they need to do is say a prayer and that's it. Christianity is not a little one-time prayer. It is a lifestyle of complete surrender to Jesus. We are selling children short if we do not challenge them to make Jesus Lord—the Boss of their lives. Christianity is not fun and games and happily ever after. Christianity is taking up our cross and following Him (see Mt. 16:24). We are misleading children if we tell them salvation is free. Yes, it is free, but it costs us everything. It will cost us our lives. When we give our lives to Jesus, they are no longer ours.

At those post-altar call sessions I also speak to the children about God's big plan for their lives. I get them to stretch out their hands to the sides as far as they can. God's plan is *big*! Then I tell them my favorite story of how a child led me, how a child showed me how big God's plan is for us.

Jeremiah Oswald—A Living Object Lesson

But seek ye first the kingdom of God, and His righteousness; and all these things shall be added unto you (Matthew 6:33).

Jeremiah Oswald received Jesus as his Savior when he was five years old. When Jeremiah was nine years old, someone told him that God had a big plan for his life. Someone taught Matthew 6:33, and Jeremiah believed it. Around that same time, at nine years of age, Jeremiah saw a vision of himself preaching to a group of children. He felt that God was calling him to be a Children's Pastor. That little boy knew what God wanted him to do, and he started doing it. He spent the majority of his spare time seeking first the Kingdom of God. He put seeking God ahead of Rollerblading and riding his bike and playing video games.

I met Jeremiah when he was 12 years of age. I was his Children's Pastor back in Evangel Temple in Montgomery. Every Sunday Jeremiah was there, helping me. He helped set up and clean up. He helped everywhere that he could throughout the meeting. Jeremiah was a blessing to me.

On the floor one day, as we were cleaning up after Children's Church, I saw one of the cloth bags we used for collecting the offering. Just for fun I put it over my hand and started talking with it as though it were a puppet. Three days later Jeremiah came and showed me a sketch of "Ollie the Offering Bag." Three weeks later he gave me the first Ollie that he ever made. I still have it in my office. I show it every night to the children who come back with me after the altar call as yet another object lesson.

Soon after that, Jeremiah started a company called Kingdom Creations, and made many more Ollies. Then he started making props for puppets— guitars, drums, and other musical instruments for puppets to "play." Jeremiah enhanced the "tear-apart-devil-doll," which has body parts attached with Velcro. Recently, Jeremiah added a full-body puppet costume to his collection. He now has people who work for him making the puppet props and costumes. He travels quite extensively, showing the products and making sales.

When I turned 16, I wasn't seeking first the Kingdom of God; I was seeking first the steering wheel. The first thing I did when I turned 16 was to rush out, get my driver's license, and jump behind the wheel of a car. When Jeremiah turned 16, he was too busy seeking first the Kingdom of God to do that. But by the time he was 17, Jeremiah bought his first car. He paid cash.

Jeremiah needed a car because he moved to Tulsa, Oklahoma, to continue studying to be a Children's Pastor. It was a very busy year for Jeremiah because he went to two schools. He graduated from high school at the age of 18 and graduated from Bible College three days later.

Now, at the age of 20, Jeremiah Oswald ministers to children full time. Kingdom Creations is a thriving business. Jeremiah is thinking about buying a house soon. He will pay cash for it.

I love telling Jeremiah's story to the children who respond to the evening altar calls at Brownsville. His testimony is very faith-building for the children. It is also very challenging. I tell them, "Jeremiah decided when he was just a little boy that he would seek first the Kingdom of God. Jeremiah didn't play games with God; he was serious. And God has blessed Jeremiah. God has a *big* plan for your life, too."

I love object lessons. Jeremiah Oswald has been a living object lesson to me personally. God has used Jeremiah in my life to teach me that, yes, children can minister. God has shown me how important it is to speak the truth to children and to challenge them to be sold out for God, *now*. And Jeremiah taught me these things, not by saying them, but by *living* them.

Remember now thy Creator in the days of thy youth... (Ecclesiastes 12:1).

Let no man despise thy youth: but be thou an example of the believers, in word, in conversation, in charity, in spirit, in faith, in purity (1 Timothy 4:12).

Our Daughter, Casey

Numerous times God has used our daughter, Casey, to teach us some spiritual lesson. During a recent family discussion, we were talking about how little time we had been able to spend with each other. Casey quietly asked, "I wonder how Jonathan Edward's family felt when he spent so much time in revival? I wonder if they ever complained?" Over and over again Casey has shown insight, wisdom, and discernment far beyond her years.

In August of 1996 Casey decided to start a T-shirt business to raise money for us to charter a bus and take 50 children to camp the following summer. She needed to raise $5,000. We had T-shirts printed using a concept the Lord had given me and set up the table. Now, we definitely have the advantage of thousands of people as possible consumers, but the Lord has blessed Casey's business beyond all our expectations. She has added more T-shirts and other items to her table. At the time of this writing, Casey's profits have exceeded anything we had thought possible. The money will be used to finance our upcoming weekly inner city outreach and go toward the purchase of a bus for the church.

Casey has run this venture completely by herself. She does all the accounting, ordering, etc. God has used this experience to help bring clarity regarding Casey's future. She has always been good at math and organizing things; now Casey knows this goes beyond a natural gifting. She knows now that God has placed a call on her life in the area of business and church administration. His blessing has been unmistakable.

As an important aside here, let me tell you my philosophy of financing Children's Ministry. I believe that churches need to highly esteem the Children's Ministry department and cover all related costs from the church budget. Having fund raisers, having boys and girls going door to door trying to raise money for Children's Ministry, is something I abhor.

Some churches take the approach of, "If you want Children's Ministry, then you make it happen." They end up with a group of untrained people trying to accomplish a ministry with no resources. Pastors and church leaders *say* that they want a dynamic ministry to children, but I believe that they are merely doing "lip service" until they are willing to put forth the financial resources needed to accomplish the task.

Jesus placed high value upon children. Matthew 10:42 says that even if we give a cup of water to a child, we will be rewarded. Several times throughout the Gospels, Jesus said that when we receive and welcome a child, we are receiving and welcoming Him. (See Matthew 18:5; Mark 9:37; Luke 9:48.) If you receive a prophet, the Bible says you will receive a prophet's reward (see Mt. 10:41). When we receive a child, we receive God's reward.

I have heard it said that when a church extends hospitality toward children—when it determines to provide quality care and facilities for them—God looks after the bills. God Himself will pick up the tab.

Pastor Vann and Mrs. Dana as Living Object Lessons

I strongly encourage married couples to be involved together in the ministry to children. It is constantly amazing to me the sense of stability that comes to Children's Church just because Mrs. Dana is there. She generally sits at the back and only comes up to the front when she wants to speak specifically to the children or to help with the altar ministry. Otherwise, she stays at the back to intercede for the meeting.

The children and I both know that when Mrs. Dana comes forward, she has something important to say—she has a Word from the Lord. When I see that woman start walking up the center aisle, I get out of the way and hand her the microphone.

The children love watching Dana and I interact; they love it when we love each other. Sometimes I bring Mrs. Dana flowers on Sunday morning. It may be just a 49 cent rose I picked up at the local grocery, but Pastor Vann brought it to Mrs. Dana. The boys and girls really enjoy watching us show affection and tease each other. Many of these children do not come from loving families. Many of them have never seen Mom and Dad do anything except argue and fight. They have never seen a godly relationship modeled for them.

From time to time I use something of Dana's from home for an object lesson. One example is her heavy cut-glass bowl. It was probably inexpensive, but to the boys and girls it looks like a valuable crystal dish. I held that bowl up at Children's Church recently, making some point in my lesson. Suddenly, I stopped and said, "Uh-oh. Mrs. Dana, I forgot to ask if I could use your crystal dish."

The boys and girls immediately turned and looked at Mrs. Dana to see her reaction. They were going nuts because Pastor Vann had blown it again. Mrs. Dana smiled a forgiving smile and said it was okay. I promised to be real careful with her dish. As the lesson progressed, I almost dropped the bowl a few times. The boys and girls loved it. Would Mrs. Dana get angry? No, there she was again with that "I-wish-you-would-be-more-careful-but-I-love-you-anyway" kind of expression on her face.

One day I brought in the lamps from our bedside tables. They are pretty little lamps that belonged to Dana's grandmother. She probably got them at a discount store, but to the boys and girls they look like priceless antiques. I began using the lamps in my lesson, when again I stopped and said, "Uh-oh. Mrs. Dana, I forgot to ask if I could use these lamps. I know they are special to you because they belonged to your grandmother. I should have asked your permission. I'm sorry, Mrs. Dana. It would have been more appropriate if I had checked with you first." The boys and girls watched

Dana's expression closely. There she was, smiling her forgiving smile.

We do that kind of interaction regularly. When the children watch us loving and treating each other with kindness, it is like wonderful, healing medicine for many of them. Dana and I can be the positive demonstration of marriage that they may not otherwise have. We pray that our relationship is one that they can look at for a role model in instances where their own family is a poor example.

The children watch not only Dana's and my interaction, but also the relationship we have with our children. Our daughters, Casey, Molly, and Whitney are all involved in some area of Children's Ministry. Our baby son, Joshua Vann, is also a focus of attention and blessing for the children. We call him "Mini Vann." Joshua is now a year-and-half old, and Mrs. Dana recently announced at Children's Church that another little member will be added to our family in a few months. The boys and girls went crazy when she announced that. Three hundred and fifty children are all having a new baby!

The children of Kingdom Kids love all over our family; it's like we are theirs. And we are.

Jacob Green—Our Twelve-Year-Old Elder

This is a true saying, If a man desire the office of a bishop [elder], he desireth a good work. A bishop then must be blameless, the husband of one wife, vigilant, sober, of good behavior, given to hospitality, apt to teach; not given to wine, no striker, not greedy of filthy lucre; but patient, not a brawler, not covetous (1 Timothy 3:1-3).

Is any sick among you? let him call for the elders of the church; and let them pray over him, anointing him with oil in the name of the Lord (James 5:14).

Another child who has been like a living object lesson to me is Jacob Green, the 12-year-old elder of Kingdom Kids. You know what an elder is, don't you? Typically, an elder is an old guy of the church who prays for the sick. I used to be the Children's Church elder. I was the oldest and I had the grayest hair. But I have not seen God use me in the area of healing.

Jacob Green is anointed by God to pray for the sick and see them recover. A little girl came to one of our services who was almost blind. Even though she wore very thick glasses, most things were totally blurry to her. In this service Jacob prayed for that little girl and she was totally healed. Jacob is a boy whose life is a strong Christian example. His hair isn't gray, but it's so blond it almost looks white. I made him my elder. He was 11 years old at the time. As far as I can see, Jacob falls short on only one scriptural requirement for an elder as laid out in First Timothy 3—he's not the husband of one wife, But of course, he's never even been a husband!

Jacob prays for the sick every Sunday morning. We even have adults coming from the sanctuary to get Jacob to pray for them. God is using him powerfully.

We have many children who are believing God for miraculous healings. I had little Amber come up and ask me to pray that her teeth would be straightened. Now, I have faith for "boo-boos" and colds to go away, but I have difficulty believing God to straighten teeth, especially after I had just spent $6,000 getting braces for two of our daughters! I said, "Amber, do you mean to tell me that I just wasted my money?!" She said, "Well, Pastor Vann, if God can open the eyes of the blind, He can surely straighten teeth." I said, "Well, let me agree with *your* faith!" And I called Jacob over to help us.

That is the kind of children we are beginning to see— boys and girls who have a strong foundation in their lives, children who know who they are in Christ.

At the same time came the disciples unto Jesus, saying, Who is the greatest in the kingdom of heaven? And Jesus called a little child unto Him, and set him in the midst of them (Matthew 18:1-2).

I like to compare people to pipes that the Holy Spirit wants to flow through. Many of us are so corroded and plugged up with sin—with hurt, bitterness, and unforgiveness; or perhaps with dead religious tradition—that our pipes are blocked. The Holy Spirit is on top, pouring into us, but all that comes out is a little trickle. As we learn to deal with sin and allow God to cleanse us, our pipes will allow a clear flow of the Holy Spirit through us to people around us.

I have come to the conclusion that God wants to use children because they are like clean pipes. They haven't gotten full of all the junk that we have. I believe that the Lord wants to use children today as living object lessons. He wants to again set a child in our midst and use that child, those children, to teach us powerful truths of His Kingdom.

Chapter 9

All Around Worship

Let everything that hath breath praise the Lord. Praise ye the Lord (Psalm 150:6).

When talking to the congregation one night, Brownsville's worship leader, Lindell Cooley, stated, "The Bible says, 'Let every thing that hath breath praise the Lord'; it does not say that everything that has breath can *worship* the Lord. We have to know Him in order to worship Him."

That was very inspiring to me. I knew it was a concept that would help children understand the difference between praise and worship. I often tell them that this means even flies can praise the Lord! Even frogs can praise the Lord! Every living thing that breathes can praise the Lord— BUT, *not* everything that breathes can *worship* the Lord. The only way we can truly worship the Lord is to know Him. Worship comes from a relationship with God.

I say, "Some of you boys and girls here today have been dancing around and having a great time during our warm-up praise songs. But when it comes time to worship, what will you be doing then? Will you close your eyes and lift up your hands?" I tell them how praise songs mainly focus on what God has done, can do, or will do for us. Worship songs focus more on who He *is*. Worship songs say, "You are Lord; I need You, Lord; I want You more than anything else in the world."

Some of the boys and girls may say, either verbally or with their body language, "I don't feel like worshiping the Lord today." I tell them that is exactly the time when they need to worship Him the most! I teach the children that worship is a decision. During praise time, I *make* children get involved. But during worship, I let them sit down if they want to do so. I challenge their attitudes by saying something like, "I could make you stand up. I could come over and grab your arms and lift up your hands, but that would be an unacceptable sacrifice to the Lord because it wouldn't be from your heart." I tell them that if they are having trouble worshiping God, it is probably because they don't know who He is. When people of any age have an understanding of who God is and what He has done for them, worship is a natural response.

I talk to the boys and girls about Jesus' death on the cross. While He was hanging there, the sun refused to shine and the earth began to quake. A line went from the bottom of that cross up to the temple steps right through to the Most Holy Place and split the big, heavy curtain there from top to bottom. Before that curtain was split, we could not go in there. We were not holy enough to go into that place. Many of the priests in those days were not holy enough to go in there, and they died if they tried to.

But when Jesus was hung on the cross, His death split that big, heavy curtain. Now He's saying, "Okay, come on in! I have taken your sin and now you are clean through Me. Come on in to My Most Holy Place!"

"But how do I get there?" the boys and girls may ask. I reply, "You get there by lifting your hands to the Lord. Forget there is anybody in the room but you and God. Go on into the Most Holy Place and kneel at the feet of Jesus. I believe you can go so close that you'll even be able to smell His wonderful fragrance. Even if you don't know the song we are singing, don't worry about it. Jesus is listening to your heart. Just close your eyes and rest in Him."

Marita McKee, whose beautiful little face is on the front cover of this book, believes me when I teach the children about worship. Let me tell you, that little girl has been some places with the Lord. I think she has been to the Throne of God, and around behind!

Second Corinthians 13:5 tells us to examine our hearts to see if our faith is true and real. I encourage the children to look inside and find out where they are at with God. Do they really know Him, or are they just at church because their parents know Him? Do they really know Him, or do they just know *about* Him?

I enjoy telling the boys and girls about the church in Korea where Dr. Yonggi Cho is pastor. I have heard the people there love to worship so much that the ushers have to ring a bell to get the congregation to stop worshiping long enough to take up the offering. That sounds like the perfect church to me. I could pastor that church. I go in and turn on the lights and air conditioner, then ring a bell when it gets to be offering time.

This really is my longing for Children's Church. I want us to go in, get all the preliminary things done, and worship God the rest of the time. I'm talking about the most perfect of curriculums. Give an object lesson, a Bible story, a memory verse, take an offering, and then worship God for the remainder of the meeting. It would be the easiest schedule in the world to put together! And that is what I do! I plan my Sunday morning outline around worship. I try to lay things out in a way in which the Holy Spirit can move in and take over—whenever and however He wants.

Sometimes, when the children are really keen to enter the Throne Room and just spend time with God, I stand on the platform and tear up my schedule. The children shout and cheer. We are about to have *church*!

On a recent Sunday morning, Cathy Wood spent time with us at Kingdom Kids. Cathy is a member of our church who does most of the photography. As a result of her visit, she put six pages of pictures on her website a few days later, along with the following article. I include it in this chapter because it really describes what has been happening as we've centered our meetings all around worship.

Yesterday at Children's Church (written by Cathy Wood on her website, www.victorious.com/Sister Wood, October 17, 1997. Used by permission.)

"Yesterday I went to Children's Church at Brownsville Assembly of God. In this service I got a lot more than I expected. Having photographed the children once before about a year ago, I still had the memory of their sweet faces as they sincerely worshipped the Lord as deeply as any adult I had ever seen. The first time I went in, I mainly photographed from the girls' side of the room. This day I decided to station myself on the boys' side even though I thought they might be silly and not as serious as the girls. WRONG!!!!....

"...As the worship team and musicians went to the platform and began playing, children immediately got up from their seats and went to the altar steps or laid right on the floor, faces into the carpet. Some curled into balls in the aisles beside their chairs. There was no working to get into the mood of worship. The hunger to go to the Throne Room was instantaneous. Apparently most of these children go there regularly. Before even the first song was over, many had those gentle shivers we see in the adults as the Lord moves on them in the big church. Some were 'crunching' in intercession. Some were on their knees, arms lifted, eyes closed, faces aimed to heaven as they rocked back and forth. They seemed to be in another place, and content to stay there. One little boy was praying with his hands in a boxing motion as he clinched his eyes shut and pounded down any principality that would come between him and his God.

"Oh...I have a lump in my throat and a gallon of tears behind my eyes as I recall the beauty of this service. I have felt like jelly on the inside all day yesterday and today after having been there with those children. I sat on the floor most of the worship time in awe.... Two young girls were twirling and dancing before the Lord in the very back. I turned to look up the center aisle toward the platform and the whole center aisle was strewn with children mostly face down. Parents that were observing were in tears, worshipping the Lord too. Wall workers (monitors) leaned against the walls, faces buried in their hands, some sobbing themselves...."

Let me share with you what had happened, which preceded the children's incredible response that morning. Jennifer Tisdale, whose father, Eddie, had kept inviting me to

Brownsville back in the first chapter, is a college student in Pensacola. Both Jennifer and her father stand out to me as exemplary worshipers. I invited Jennifer to come in and speak to the children about worship.

What God gave her to share was a beautiful illustration that every child could relate to. She told them how when boys and girls go to someone's house they do not know, they usually feel shy. Sometimes, while everyone is in the living room, they will hide behind their parents. But the longer they stay, the more comfortable they begin to feel.

Then perhaps one of the children who lives in that house comes over and says, "Hey, do you want to come and see my room?" As the young visitor goes back to that child's room, as he sees the toys and gets to know the other child, they become friends. Then, every time he goes to visit, he wants to go to that child's room, because now they are best friends.

Jennifer went on to say that going to church is like going into the living room. Jesus wants us to come into His room. When we come into His room, that is when we will get to know Him. As we spend time in His room, Jesus becomes our best friend.

In her article about that Sunday morning, Cathy Wood mentioned how, as soon as worship began, numerous children headed for the altar. Many Sunday mornings I don't need to give an invitation for the boys and girls to come forward at the end of the service; they have allowed God to deal with their hearts throughout our worship time. Some children go back and forth several times during worship as the Lord convicts them of areas in their lives.

Not all of the children enter in so beautifully. We have a number of boys and girls who still want to play around and not get serious with God. But that number is growing smaller. We also have many visiting children each week. They have come from extremely varied backgrounds, and many of them have never seen children loving God like this. These visitors are not used to seeing other children all over the floor, sincerely crying out to the Lord. They aren't used to the weeping and the bodily manifestations of intercession. They have never seen anyone worshiping God with all his or her might.

That is very sad when you pause to consider it...children surprised to see others zealous in their love for God. This should be normal Christianity! Our children should be used to it! The greatest commandment God has given to us is to love Him with all our heart, soul, mind, and strength.

And thou shalt love the Lord thy God with all thy heart, and with all thy soul, and with all thy mind, and with all thy strength: this is the first commandment (Mark 12:30).

I like to tell the boys and girls about how King David worshiped the Lord with all his being. He danced and jumped and made so much noise that he got too warm and decided to worship in his underwear! (See Second Samuel 6:14.) King David didn't care what other people thought. He wanted to worship as loud and hard and fast as he could!

I take a few moments to speak to the children who are observing but not entering in. I say things like, "Listen, these children here are spending time with God. And you know what? They don't care one little bit what you think about them! These children are serious about God. Some of them are responding to something He is speaking to their hearts. Others of them are praying. They are interceding—they are calling out to God—for *you*! God wants you to spend time with Him. God wants you to talk to Him."

I love to see children go off to some place in the Throne Room. But my heart still yearns that for *every* child to go to there, too. Sometimes I will say, "We're going to sing one more song. If you haven't worshiped the Lord yet today, here is one more chance." We offer one more opportunity. We ask the Holy Spirit to draw every child closer to Him.

We don't beg; it's more like pleading. I want so much for them to taste and see how very good the Lord is (see Ps. 34:8). I know that one minute in His presence will do far more for them than anything I could ever teach them; it will do more than any puppet show or object lesson we could present to them.

There are a lot of truths we can apply in our time of worship with children. We can teach them the scriptural principles of clapping, lifting hands, dancing, bowing, etc., but we must go beyond teaching truth to helping them apply it. The application of that truth can best be imparted as we ourselves are living examples. The Father is looking for that kind of worship.

But the hour cometh, and now is, when the true worshippers shall worship the Father in spirit and in truth: for the Father seeketh such to worship Him. God is a Spirit: and they that worship Him must worship Him in spirit and in truth (John 4:23-24).

An environment where children fall in love with Jesus can be created. It can be created by the Holy Spirit if we will give Him control. It can be created as we ourselves model and demonstrate how to love Jesus. This is the challenge I set before our worship team. They can simply go through a series of religious motions, or they can demonstrate joy, adoration, and abandonment to the Lord in true worship. I believe that many of our children truly are worshiping in spirit and in truth, and it is mainly the result of the musicians who are leading them. Our band is called and anointed by God. We have seen sovereign supply of both musicians and equipment.

God put our band of 12- to 16-year-olds together. Justin Bloodworth had always loved to play drums, but the only thing he had to play was the dashboard of his mama's car. So, we prayed in a set of drums! In my former days I myself played drums in a rock and roll band. I will never be as good a drummer as Justin is. In less than one year God has raised him up to be the backup for the studio drummer in the sanctuary. He plays for every Wednesday nights service.

Christopher Stanton had a talent to play the keyboard and lead worship. Together he and I picked out a keyboard and prayed it in. We had prayed for just a week and a half when our church administrator called me into his office. "Do you know anything about a keyboard for Children's Church?" he asked. "I sure do!" I said, "We're praying for one." "Well, you can quit praying," he said, handing me a check for $2,000 which someone had brought in and designated for that purpose. It was the right amount—almost to the penny.

When Christopher hits the first keys on that keyboard Sunday mornings, the glory of God fills the room. Christopher has been studying Lindell Cooley, Brownsville's worship leader, ever since the revival started. His touch on the keyboard is exactly the same as Lindell's. His posture, his style of worship is a replica of Lindell's. It is both beautiful and powerful to see. He has patterned himself after the demonstration of a true worshiper.

Some Sundays we have "gotten stuck" in worship. We get there and the children just won't leave. Now, I don't know about you, but getting children stuck in worship is my idea of success. The ultimate goal we have for every children's meeting is to get the boys and girls into God's presence—where they can feel His nearness and hear His voice. When we get to that place, I want to let the children stay there as long as possible.

That might mean cutting back other things we had planned. It might mean canceling the puppet skit that the team had prepared. It might mean not getting to sing that special song the band had rehearsed. My young workers have no problem with that kind of thing. They know that the Holy Spirit is the Boss on Sunday morning and what He says goes. If there are things we don't get to on a certain morning, we usually put them into the next week's plan.

Everything we do is centered around worshiping Jesus. It is our goal. It is the heartbeat of our Children's Ministry. People ask me about future goals: Where to from here?

I'll tell you where we want to go from here. We want to go places in God. We want to go forward into all the new things He has planned for us. What we have experienced has been exceeding, abundantly above and beyond what we had expected or dared to imagine (see Eph. 3:20). But we have a sense that the visitation of God in these days has only just begun. For the past several years, the cry of Brownsville Assembly of God has been, "More, Lord!"

*I am very excited and interested to find out what **more** will look like.*

Chapter 10

More, Lord

And blessed be His glorious name for ever: and let the whole earth be filled with His glory; Amen, and Amen (Psalm 72:19).

And one [angel] cried unto another, and said, Holy, holy, holy, is the Lord of hosts: the whole earth is full of His glory (Isaiah 6:3).

For the earth shall be filled with the knowledge of the glory of the Lord, as the waters cover the sea (Habakkuk 2:14).

Thy kingdom come. Thy will be done in earth, as it is in heaven (Matthew 6:10).

These Scriptures are not just wishful thinking about some far-off day. *This is what God wants to do.* Jesus told His disciples to pray for His Kingdom to come and for His will to be done on the earth in the same way it is done in Heaven. There is no sickness or sadness in Heaven. There is no crime or hatred or depression. *Think about it—the Kingdom of God coming to this world and the glory of God filling the earth. What will that look like?!*

Several months ago I saw a vision of a mother pushing her little boy in a wheelchair into Children's Church. I looked closer and realized that the boy had no foot on one of his legs. I looked up and said, "Lord, there is nothing there to work with!" Then, in my vision, I saw that little boy push his own wheelchair out the door. As I watched, I heard the Holy Spirit say, "Greater things than these shall you see."

Verily, verily, I say unto you, He that believeth on Me, the works that I do shall he do also; and greater works than these shall he do; because I go unto My Father (John 14:12).

For years the Church has been crying out for a mighty move of God. We have seen some evidence; we have seen a trickle. As we continue to cry out, "More, Lord!" *more* is exactly what we will see—more miracles, more signs and wonders, more of God's Kingdom filling the earth.

There is an intercessor in our church who prays for me regularly, and I have come to respect him as a man who hears from God. Before we took those 50 children to camp last summer, he came to me and described the camp in detail, although he had never been there. Then he went on to encourage me about the difficult week we were about to face. Everything he told me came to pass.

Around that same time, he received another word from the Lord for us. He said, "I saw Brownsville as a small dot in the bottom of the Grand Canyon. Flowing right through the church was a small stream. At the top of the canyon I saw a dam—and the dam was made up of children. Behind the dam of children I saw a raging flood."

We feel that the Lord is saying that children will usher in the next outpouring. Something that far surpasses anything we have seen thus far is about to break forth.

Recently our church has had a new and increased feeling of expectancy. It is similar to what we felt during the days prior to Father's Day, 1995. Another wave is coming. God is about to do yet another new thing. It's in the air, and the level of anticipation is again so great that it is almost something we can touch.

The anticipation that I feel personally is that God is going to open the floodgates through the children. What we have seen up to this point in time has been like a little creek. I thought it was a river, but now I realize that it has just been a creek.

There's more. The time is coming when we will see the miracles. We will see the healings. We will see the dead raised and the blind walk and the deaf hear. This world needs to witness the power of God manifested through His people. God doesn't just want to pour out His Spirit on a few churches! He wants the whole earth to be filled with His glory! He wants His Kingdom to come and His will to be done right now, right here on the earth—just like it is in Heaven!

The bit of earth near Brownsville has experienced some of that glory. The community surrounding our church is slowly but surely being touched by the revival. People are beginning to be reached and you can see the difference. The houses are getting painted. The yards are being cleaned up. The whole look of our neighborhood is taking on a new appearance.

We have been earnestly praying and seeking the Lord for ways to reach our city. We don't want to try to keep revival within the church walls. How sad it would be if people from the nations of the world literally lined up at our door, but the families who live down the street were not affected.

We are almost ready to launch an inner-city outreach to children. Students from the School of Ministry will be taking key roles in this outreach, and it will be financed through our daughter Casey's T-shirt business. Our plan is to set up a truck with a stage and sound system in at least two different neighborhoods (to begin with) every Saturday. We will present the gospel in creative ways and, as God's glory indeed covers this part of the earth, I believe we will minister in creative miracles as well—in people's hearts, minds, bodies, and families.

I believe that extensive inner-city outreach must not begin until we have thoroughly counted the cost and done adequate preparation. We need to make a long-term commitment to the people who live there; they need to know that we will come back faithfully every week. I feel that this is especially important to the children of these areas. Throughout their young lives those boys and girls have faced constant disappointment and abandonment. We want to demonstrate the faithfulness of the Lord to them. We want to earn their trust so that they can in turn trust Jesus. This will only happen as we spend time with them on a regular and consistent basis.

Our plan is to conduct our Children's Ministry in the inner city in much the same way that we do on Sunday mornings. These, too, will be "Kingdom Kids"—they will do the work of the ministry with adult overseers. As we see leadership capabilities in them, the boys and girls themselves will be given areas of responsibility. They will take attendance, greet and usher, lead the singing, do the puppet presentations, and monitor behavior of the other children.

I believe the children of the inner city will become our next "children of revival." They will experience the power and presence of Jesus and, as a result, they will lead their peers and parents to Him.

The Amplified Bible puts Habakkuk 2:2 this way: "...Write the vision and engrave it so plainly upon tablets that everyone who passes may [be able to] read [it easily and quickly] as he hastens by."

My prayer is that this book has been easy for you to read. As you have "hastened by" and read it in the midst of your busy life, I pray that it has both blessed and challenged you. I also pray that the easy and quick words of these pages will have had, and will continue to have, a deep and eternal effect upon your heart. I pray that the way you look at the little members of your church has been, and will continue to be, forever impacted.

I have a deep awareness that this book may very well serve to soften the hearts of many people toward the new things God is desiring to do in His Church. May you, dear reader, respond to the testimonies of these "children of revival," and *let them lead you* into greater realms of adventure with Him.

References

Brown, Michael. *Let No One Deceive You* (Shippensburg, PA: Destiny Image Publishers, 1997).

Layton, Dian. *Soldiers With Little Feet* (Shippensburg, PA: Destiny Image Publishers, 1989).

"Managing the Revival," Destiny Image *Digest* (Winter, 1997; Vol. 5, No. 1), pp. 37-38.

Walters, David. *Children Aflame* (Macon, GA: Good News Publishing, 1995).

Destiny Image
Revival Books

LET NO ONE DECEIVE YOU
by Dr. Michael L. Brown.
No one is knowingly deceived. Everyone assumes it's "the other guy" who is off track. So when people dispute the validity of current revivals, how do you know who is right? In this book Dr. Michael Brown takes a look at current revivals and at the arguments critics are using to question their validity. After examining Scripture, historical accounts of past revivals, and the fruits of the current movements, Dr. Brown comes to a logical conclusion: God's Spirit is moving. *Let No One Deceive You!*
ISBN 1-56043-693-X $10.99p

THE GOD MOCKERS
And Other Messages From the Brownsville Revival
by Stephen Hill.
Hear the truth of God as few men have dared to tell it! In his usual passionate and direct manner, Evangelist Stephen Hill directs people to an uncompromised Christian life of holiness. The messages in this book will burn through every hindrance that keeps you from going further in God!
ISBN 1-56043-691-3 $9.99p

IT'S TIME
by Richard Crisco.
"We say that 'Generation X' does not know what they are searching for in life. But we are wrong. They know what they desire. We, as the Church, are the ones without a revelation of what they need." It is time to stop entertaining our youth with pizza parties and start training an army for God. Find out in this dynamic book how the Brownsville youth have exploded with revival power...affecting the surrounding schools and communities!
ISBN 1-56043-690-5 $9.99p

A TOUCH OF GLORY
by Lindell Cooley.
This book was written for the countless "unknowns" who, like Lindell Cooley, are being plucked from obscurity for a divine work of destiny. Here Lindell, the worship leader of the Brownsville Revival, tells of his own journey from knowing God's hand was upon him to trusting Him. The key to personal revival is a life-changing encounter with the living God. There is no substitute for a touch of His glory.
ISBN 1-56043-689-1 $9.99p

Available at your local Christian bookstore.
nternet: http://www.reapernet.com

Destiny Image
Revival Books

PORTAL IN PENSACOLA
by Renee DeLoriea.
What is happening in Pensacola, Florida? Why are people from all over the world streaming to one church in this city? The answer is simple: ***Revival!*** For more than a year, Renee DeLoriea has lived in the midst of the revival at Brownsville Assembly of God. *Portal in Pensacola* is her firsthand account of this powerful move of the Spirit that is illuminating and transforming the lives of thousands!
ISBN 1-56043-189-X $9.99p

THE POWER OF BROKENNESS
by Don Nori.
Accepting Brokenness is a must for becoming a true vessel of the Lord, and is a stepping-stone to revival in our hearts, our homes, and our churches. Brokenness alone brings us to the wonderful revelation of how deep and great our Lord's mercy really is. Join this companion who leads us through the darkest of nights. Discover the *Power of Brokenness*.
ISBN 1-56043-178-4 $9.99p

WHEN THE HEAVENS ARE BRASS
by John Kilpatrick.
Pastor John Kilpatrick wanted something more. He began to pray, but it seemed like the heavens were brass. The lessons he learned over the years helped birth a mighty revival in Brownsville Assembly of God that is sweeping through this nation and the world. The dynamic truths in this book could birth life-changing revival in your own life and ministry!
ISBN 1-56043-190-3 $9.99p

WHITE CANE RELIGION
And Other Messages From the Brownsville Revival
by Stephen Hill.
In less than two years, Evangelist Stephen Hill has won nearly 100,000 to Christ while preaching repentance, forgiveness, and the power of the blood in what has been called "The Brownsville Revival" in Pensacola, Florida. Experience the anointing of the best of this evangelist's life-changing revival messages in this dynamic book!
ISBN 1-56043-186-5 $9.99p

Available at your local Christian bookstore.
Internet: http://www.reapernet.com

Destiny Image
New Releases

WHEN GOD STRIKES THE MATCH
by Dr. Harvey R. Brown, Jr.
A noted preacher, college administrator, and father of an "all-American" family—what more could a man want? But when God struck the match that set Harvey Brown ablaze, it ignited a passion for holiness and renewal in his heart that led him into a head-on encounter with the consuming fire of God.
ISBN 0-7684-1000-2 $9.99p

THE LOST ART OF INTERCESSION
by Jim W. Goll.
How can you experience God's anointing power as a result of your own prayer? Learn what the Moravians discovered during their 100-year prayer Watch. They sent up prayers; God sent down His power. Jim Goll, who ministers worldwide through a teaching and prophetic ministry, urges us to heed Jesus' warning to "watch." Through Scripture, the Moravian example, and his own prayer life, Jim Goll proves that "what goes up must come down."
ISBN 1-56043-697-2 $9.99p

WORSHIP: THE PATTERN OF THINGS IN HEAVEN
by Joseph L. Garlington.
Joseph Garlington, a favorite Promise Keepers' speaker and worship leader, delves into Scripture to reveal worship and praise from a Heaven's-eye view. Learn just how deep, full, and anointed God intends our worship to be.
ISBN 1-56043-195-4 $9.99p

Available at your local Christian bookstore.

Internet: http://www.reapernet.com